50 Japanese Cake Recipes for Home

By: Kelly Johnson

Table of Contents

- Matcha Green Tea Cake
- Japanese Cheesecake
- Black Sesame Seed Cake
- Sakura Cherry Blossom Cake
- Yuzu Citrus Cake
- Mochi Cake
- Kinako (Roasted Soybean Flour) Cake
- Red Bean (Adzuki) Cake
- Castella (Japanese Sponge Cake)
- Dorayaki (Red Bean Pancake Cake)
- Japanese Cotton Soft Cheesecake
- Hojicha (Roasted Green Tea) Cake
- Uji Matcha Roll Cake
- Melon Pan Cake
- Japanese Strawberry Shortcake
- Satsuma Imo (Japanese Sweet Potato) Cake
- Wagashi-inspired Cake
- Shingen Mochi Cake
- Mitarashi Dango (Skewered Rice Dumplings) Cake
- Wasabi Cake
- Yomogi (Japanese Mugwort) Cake
- Anmitsu Cake
- Chestnut Cake
- Dorayaki-inspired Cake
- Ichigo Daifuku (Strawberry Mochi) Cake
- Tofu Cheesecake
- Soba Cha (Buckwheat Tea) Cake
- Japanese Pumpkin (Kabocha) Cake
- Amaou Strawberry Cake
- Taiyaki-inspired Cake
- Shiroi Koibito-inspired Cake
- Kyoto Uji Matcha Cake
- Japanese Honey Castella
- Warabi Mochi Cake
- Daifuku Mochi Cake

- Kuri Kinton (Chestnut Sweet) Cake
- Kasutera (Japanese Honey Sponge Cake)
- Okinawan Sweet Potato Cake
- Ichigo Roll Cake
- Dorayaki Roll Cake
- Karinto (Japanese Fried Dough) Cake
- Zunda (Sweetened Edamame Paste) Cake
- Sata Andagi (Okinawan Donut) Cake
- Himono Cake
- Yuzu Honey Cake
- Kuzumochi Cake
- Japanese Sweet Bean Cake
- Anko (Sweet Red Bean Paste) Cake
- Yatsuhashi (Cinnamon Rice Flour Dumpling) Cake
- Yakimochi (Grilled Rice Cake) Cake

Matcha Green Tea Cake

Ingredients:

- 1 3/4 cups all-purpose flour
- 2 tablespoons matcha green tea powder
- 1 teaspoon baking powder
- 1/2 teaspoon baking soda
- 1/2 teaspoon salt
- 1/2 cup unsalted butter, softened
- 1 cup granulated sugar
- 2 large eggs
- 1 teaspoon vanilla extract
- 1 cup buttermilk

Instructions:

1. Preheat your oven to 350°F (175°C). Grease and flour a 9-inch round cake pan or line it with parchment paper.
2. In a medium bowl, whisk together the flour, matcha powder, baking powder, baking soda, and salt. Set aside.
3. In a large mixing bowl, cream together the softened butter and granulated sugar until light and fluffy.
4. Add the eggs one at a time, mixing well after each addition. Stir in the vanilla extract.
5. Gradually add the flour mixture to the wet ingredients, alternating with buttermilk, beginning and ending with the flour mixture. Mix until just combined, being careful not to overmix.
6. Pour the batter into the prepared cake pan and spread it evenly.
7. Bake in the preheated oven for 25-30 minutes, or until a toothpick inserted into the center of the cake comes out clean.
8. Remove the cake from the oven and let it cool in the pan for 10 minutes. Then, transfer the cake onto a wire rack to cool completely.
9. Once cooled, you can dust the cake with powdered sugar or frost it with your favorite icing. Enjoy your delicious Matcha Green Tea Cake!

This cake is perfect for tea time or as a delightful dessert to impress guests with its unique flavor and beautiful green color.

Japanese Cheesecake

Ingredients:

- 140g cream cheese, at room temperature
- 40g unsalted butter
- 50ml whole milk
- 4 large eggs, separated
- 1/4 teaspoon cream of tartar
- 100g granulated sugar
- 1 tablespoon lemon juice
- 60g cake flour
- 20g cornstarch
- 1/4 teaspoon salt
- Powdered sugar, for dusting

Instructions:

1. Preheat your oven to 320°F (160°C). Grease and line the bottom and sides of a 7-inch round cake pan with parchment paper.
2. In a heatproof bowl, combine the cream cheese, butter, and milk. Place the bowl over a pot of simmering water (double boiler) and stir until melted and smooth. Remove from heat and let it cool slightly.
3. Separate the egg yolks and whites into two separate bowls. Add the egg yolks one at a time to the cream cheese mixture, stirring well after each addition. Stir in the lemon juice.
4. Sift together the cake flour, cornstarch, and salt. Gradually add this dry mixture to the cream cheese mixture, stirring until smooth.
5. In a clean mixing bowl, whisk the egg whites with cream of tartar until foamy. Gradually add the granulated sugar, a little at a time, while continuing to whisk. Whisk until stiff peaks form.
6. Gently fold the egg whites into the cream cheese mixture in three batches, using a spatula. Be careful not to deflate the mixture too much.
7. Pour the batter into the prepared cake pan and smooth the top with a spatula.
8. Place the cake pan into a larger baking dish. Fill the larger baking dish with hot water halfway up the sides of the cake pan (this helps create a moist baking environment).
9. Bake in the preheated oven for 60-70 minutes, or until the top is lightly golden and the center of the cake is set. The cake should jiggle slightly when gently shaken.
10. Turn off the oven and leave the cake in the oven with the door slightly ajar for about 30 minutes to cool gradually.
11. Remove the cake from the oven and let it cool completely in the cake pan. Once cooled, dust the top with powdered sugar.
12. Carefully remove the cake from the pan, slice, and serve. Enjoy your delicious Japanese Cheesecake!

This Japanese Cheesecake is renowned for its soft, fluffy texture and delicate flavor, making it a delightful treat for any occasion.

Black Sesame Seed Cake

Ingredients:

- 1 cup black sesame seeds
- 1/2 cup unsalted butter, softened
- 3/4 cup granulated sugar
- 3 large eggs
- 1 teaspoon vanilla extract
- 1 cup all-purpose flour
- 1 teaspoon baking powder
- 1/4 teaspoon salt
- 1/2 cup milk

Instructions:

1. Preheat your oven to 350°F (175°C). Grease and flour a 9-inch round cake pan or line it with parchment paper.
2. In a dry skillet or frying pan, toast the black sesame seeds over medium heat for about 3-4 minutes, stirring frequently, until fragrant. Be careful not to burn them. Remove from heat and let them cool.
3. Grind the toasted black sesame seeds in a food processor or blender until finely ground. Set aside.
4. In a large mixing bowl, cream together the softened butter and granulated sugar until light and fluffy.
5. Add the eggs one at a time, mixing well after each addition. Stir in the vanilla extract.
6. In a separate bowl, whisk together the ground black sesame seeds, flour, baking powder, and salt.
7. Gradually add the dry ingredients to the wet ingredients, alternating with milk, beginning and ending with the flour mixture. Mix until just combined, being careful not to overmix.
8. Pour the batter into the prepared cake pan and spread it evenly.
9. Bake in the preheated oven for 30-35 minutes, or until a toothpick inserted into the center of the cake comes out clean.
10. Remove the cake from the oven and let it cool in the pan for 10 minutes. Then, transfer the cake onto a wire rack to cool completely.
11. Once cooled, you can dust the cake with powdered sugar or serve it plain. Enjoy your delicious Black Sesame Seed Cake!

This cake offers a delightful contrast of flavors and textures, making it a wonderful choice for those who appreciate unique and nutty desserts.

Sakura Cherry Blossom Cake

Ingredients:

- 1 cup cake flour
- 1 teaspoon baking powder
- 1/4 teaspoon salt
- 1/2 cup unsalted butter, softened
- 1 cup granulated sugar
- 3 large eggs
- 1/2 cup whole milk
- 1 teaspoon vanilla extract
- 1/2 teaspoon almond extract
- Pink food coloring (optional)
- Sakura (cherry blossom) essence or extract (available at specialty stores)

For the Frosting:

- 1/2 cup unsalted butter, softened
- 2 cups powdered sugar
- 1-2 tablespoons whole milk or cream
- 1/2 teaspoon vanilla extract
- Pink food coloring (optional)

Decoration:

- Edible cherry blossoms (sakura) for garnish (available online or in Japanese specialty stores)

Instructions:

1. **Preparation:** Preheat your oven to 350°F (175°C). Grease and flour two 9-inch round cake pans or line them with parchment paper.
2. **Dry Ingredients:** In a bowl, sift together the cake flour, baking powder, and salt. Set aside.
3. **Wet Ingredients:** In a large mixing bowl, cream together the softened butter and granulated sugar until light and fluffy.
4. **Eggs and Flavorings:** Add the eggs one at a time, mixing well after each addition. Stir in the vanilla extract, almond extract, and a few drops of sakura essence or extract to taste.
5. **Combining Mixtures:** Gradually add the dry ingredients to the wet ingredients, alternating with the milk, beginning and ending with the flour mixture. Mix until just combined. If desired, add a few drops of pink food coloring for a delicate hue.
6. **Baking:** Divide the batter evenly between the prepared cake pans. Smooth the tops with a spatula. Bake in the preheated oven for 25-30 minutes, or until a toothpick inserted into the center of the cakes comes out clean.
7. **Cooling:** Remove the cakes from the oven and let them cool in the pans for 10 minutes. Then, transfer them to a wire rack to cool completely.
8. **Frosting:** While the cakes are cooling, prepare the frosting. In a mixing bowl, beat the softened butter until creamy. Gradually add the powdered sugar, alternating with the milk or cream, until

the desired consistency is reached. Beat in the vanilla extract and pink food coloring, if using, until smooth and fluffy.
9. **Assembly:** Once the cakes are completely cooled, place one cake layer on a serving plate or cake stand. Spread a layer of frosting over the top. Place the second cake layer on top and frost the top and sides of the cake with the remaining frosting.
10. **Decoration:** Garnish the cake with edible cherry blossoms (sakura) on top for a beautiful and authentic touch.
11. **Serve:** Slice and serve your Sakura Cherry Blossom Cake, enjoying its delicate flavors and elegant appearance.

This cake celebrates the beauty and taste of cherry blossoms, making it a perfect choice for special occasions or any time you want to savor a taste of Japan's springtime.

Yuzu Citrus Cake

Ingredients:

- 1 1/2 cups all-purpose flour
- 1 1/2 teaspoons baking powder
- 1/4 teaspoon salt
- 1/2 cup unsalted butter, softened
- 1 cup granulated sugar
- 3 large eggs
- 1/2 cup plain yogurt or sour cream
- Zest of 2 yuzu fruits (about 2 tablespoons)
- Juice of 1 yuzu fruit (about 1/4 cup)
- 1 teaspoon vanilla extract

For the Glaze:

- Juice of 1 yuzu fruit (about 1/4 cup)
- 1 cup powdered sugar

Instructions:

1. **Preparation:** Preheat your oven to 350°F (175°C). Grease and flour a 9-inch round cake pan or line it with parchment paper.
2. **Dry Ingredients:** In a bowl, sift together the flour, baking powder, and salt. Set aside.
3. **Wet Ingredients:** In a large mixing bowl, cream together the softened butter and granulated sugar until light and fluffy.
4. **Eggs and Flavorings:** Add the eggs one at a time, mixing well after each addition. Stir in the yogurt or sour cream, yuzu zest, yuzu juice, and vanilla extract.
5. **Combining Mixtures:** Gradually add the dry ingredients to the wet ingredients, mixing until just combined. Be careful not to overmix.
6. **Baking:** Pour the batter into the prepared cake pan and spread it evenly.
7. **Bake:** Bake in the preheated oven for 30-35 minutes, or until a toothpick inserted into the center of the cake comes out clean.
8. **Cooling:** Remove the cake from the oven and let it cool in the pan for 10 minutes. Then, transfer the cake onto a wire rack to cool completely.
9. **Glaze:** While the cake is cooling, prepare the glaze. In a small bowl, whisk together the yuzu juice and powdered sugar until smooth.
10. **Drizzle:** Once the cake has cooled, drizzle the yuzu glaze evenly over the top of the cake.
11. **Serve:** Slice and serve your Yuzu Citrus Cake, enjoying its bright and tangy flavors.

This cake is perfect for citrus lovers and is a refreshing treat that captures the unique essence of yuzu.

Mochi Cake

Ingredients:

- 1 pound mochiko (sweet rice flour)
- 2 1/2 cups granulated sugar
- 1 teaspoon baking powder
- 1/2 cup unsalted butter, melted and cooled
- 1 can (13.5 oz) coconut milk
- 1 can (12 oz) evaporated milk
- 5 large eggs
- 1 teaspoon vanilla extract

Instructions:

1. **Preparation:** Preheat your oven to 350°F (175°C). Grease a 9x13-inch baking dish.
2. **Dry Ingredients:** In a large bowl, whisk together the mochiko, granulated sugar, and baking powder.
3. **Wet Ingredients:** In another bowl, combine the melted butter, coconut milk, evaporated milk, eggs, and vanilla extract. Mix until well combined.
4. **Combine:** Gradually add the wet ingredients to the dry ingredients, stirring until smooth and well incorporated.
5. **Bake:** Pour the batter into the prepared baking dish and smooth the top with a spatula.
6. **Baking:** Bake in the preheated oven for 1 hour to 1 hour 15 minutes, or until the top is golden brown and a toothpick inserted into the center comes out clean.
7. **Cooling:** Remove from the oven and let the cake cool completely in the baking dish on a wire rack.
8. **Serve:** Once cooled, cut into squares and serve. Enjoy your delicious Butter Mochi Cake!

This Mochi Cake is loved for its unique chewy texture and delightful coconut flavor, making it a favorite dessert for gatherings and celebrations.

Kinako (Roasted Soybean Flour) Cake

Ingredients:

- 1 cup all-purpose flour
- 1 cup kinako (roasted soybean flour)
- 1 teaspoon baking powder
- 1/2 teaspoon baking soda
- 1/4 teaspoon salt
- 1/2 cup unsalted butter, softened
- 1 cup granulated sugar
- 2 large eggs
- 1 teaspoon vanilla extract
- 1 cup buttermilk

Instructions:

1. **Preparation:** Preheat your oven to 350°F (175°C). Grease and flour a 9-inch round cake pan or line it with parchment paper.
2. **Dry Ingredients:** In a bowl, whisk together the all-purpose flour, kinako, baking powder, baking soda, and salt. Set aside.
3. **Wet Ingredients:** In a large mixing bowl, cream together the softened butter and granulated sugar until light and fluffy.
4. **Eggs and Flavoring:** Add the eggs one at a time, mixing well after each addition. Stir in the vanilla extract.
5. **Combine Mixtures:** Gradually add the dry ingredients to the wet ingredients, alternating with buttermilk, beginning and ending with the flour mixture. Mix until just combined, being careful not to overmix.
6. **Baking:** Pour the batter into the prepared cake pan and spread it evenly.
7. **Bake:** Bake in the preheated oven for 30-35 minutes, or until a toothpick inserted into the center of the cake comes out clean.
8. **Cooling:** Remove the cake from the oven and let it cool in the pan for 10 minutes. Then, transfer the cake onto a wire rack to cool completely.
9. **Serve:** Once cooled, you can dust the top with additional kinako powder or powdered sugar if desired. Slice and serve your delicious Kinako Cake!

This cake offers a delightful nutty flavor from the kinako, making it a unique and enjoyable treat for those who appreciate Japanese flavors.

Red Bean (Adzuki) Cake

Ingredients:

- 1 cup cooked and mashed adzuki beans (canned or homemade)
- 1/2 cup unsalted butter, softened
- 1 cup granulated sugar
- 2 large eggs
- 1 teaspoon vanilla extract
- 1 1/2 cups all-purpose flour
- 1 1/2 teaspoons baking powder
- 1/4 teaspoon salt
- 1/2 cup milk

Instructions:

1. **Preparation:** Preheat your oven to 350°F (175°C). Grease and flour a 9-inch round cake pan or line it with parchment paper.
2. **Dry Ingredients:** In a bowl, whisk together the all-purpose flour, baking powder, and salt. Set aside.
3. **Wet Ingredients:** In a large mixing bowl, cream together the softened butter and granulated sugar until light and fluffy.
4. **Eggs and Flavoring:** Add the eggs one at a time, mixing well after each addition. Stir in the vanilla extract.
5. **Combine Mixtures:** Gradually add the mashed adzuki beans to the wet ingredients, mixing until well combined.
6. **Add Dry Ingredients:** Gradually add the dry ingredients to the wet ingredients, alternating with milk, beginning and ending with the flour mixture. Mix until just combined, being careful not to overmix.
7. **Baking:** Pour the batter into the prepared cake pan and spread it evenly.
8. **Bake:** Bake in the preheated oven for 30-35 minutes, or until a toothpick inserted into the center of the cake comes out clean.
9. **Cooling:** Remove the cake from the oven and let it cool in the pan for 10 minutes. Then, transfer the cake onto a wire rack to cool completely.
10. **Serve:** Once cooled, you can dust the top with powdered sugar or serve it plain. Slice and serve your delicious Red Bean Cake!

This cake offers a unique twist with its incorporation of adzuki beans, providing a delightful sweetness and texture that's perfect for any occasion.

Castella (Japanese Sponge Cake)

Ingredients:

- 6 large eggs
- 1 cup granulated sugar
- 1 cup cake flour
- 1/4 cup honey
- 1/4 cup milk
- 1/4 cup vegetable oil
- 1 teaspoon vanilla extract
- Powdered sugar, for dusting

Instructions:

1. **Preparation:** Preheat your oven to 325°F (160°C). Grease and line a 9x5 inch loaf pan with parchment paper.
2. **Egg Mixture:** In a mixing bowl, beat the eggs and sugar together with an electric mixer on high speed until pale and thick, about 10-15 minutes. The mixture should be fluffy and almost triple in volume.
3. **Adding Flour:** Sift the cake flour over the egg mixture in two additions, gently folding it in with a spatula after each addition until just combined. Be careful not to deflate the batter.
4. **Adding Honey and Liquid Ingredients:** In a small saucepan, warm the honey, milk, and vegetable oil over low heat until combined and smooth. Remove from heat and stir in the vanilla extract.
5. **Incorporate Liquid Mixture:** Gradually add the warm honey mixture to the batter, folding gently until well combined.
6. **Baking:** Pour the batter into the prepared loaf pan and tap the pan gently on the counter to remove any air bubbles. Bake in the preheated oven for 50-60 minutes, or until the top is golden brown and a toothpick inserted into the center comes out clean.
7. **Cooling:** Remove the cake from the oven and let it cool in the pan for 10 minutes. Then, transfer the cake onto a wire rack to cool completely.
8. **Dusting with Powdered Sugar:** Once cooled, dust the top of the Castella with powdered sugar.
9. **Slice and Serve:** Slice the Castella into pieces and serve. Enjoy your delicious Japanese sponge cake!

Castella is known for its soft and moist texture, making it a wonderful treat to enjoy with tea or coffee.

Dorayaki (Red Bean Pancake Cake)

Ingredients:

- 2 large eggs
- 1/2 cup granulated sugar
- 1 tablespoon honey
- 1 teaspoon vanilla extract
- 1 cup all-purpose flour
- 1/2 teaspoon baking powder
- 1/4 cup water
- Sweet red bean paste (anko), store-bought or homemade
- Vegetable oil, for cooking

Instructions:

1. **Whisk Eggs and Sugar:** In a mixing bowl, whisk together the eggs and granulated sugar until well combined and slightly frothy.
2. **Add Honey and Vanilla:** Add the honey and vanilla extract to the egg mixture, and whisk until incorporated.
3. **Sift Dry Ingredients:** In a separate bowl, sift together the all-purpose flour and baking powder.
4. **Combine Wet and Dry Ingredients:** Gradually add the flour mixture to the egg mixture, alternating with water, and whisk until smooth and no lumps remain. The batter should have a pourable consistency similar to pancake batter.
5. **Rest the Batter:** Let the batter rest for about 10-15 minutes to allow it to thicken slightly.
6. **Heat the Pan:** Heat a non-stick skillet or griddle over medium-low heat. Lightly grease the pan with vegetable oil.
7. **Cook the Pancakes:** Pour about 1/4 cup of batter onto the heated pan for each dorayaki. Cook until bubbles form on the surface of the pancake and the edges start to set, about 2-3 minutes. Flip and cook the other side for another 1-2 minutes, until golden brown and cooked through. Repeat with the remaining batter.
8. **Cooling:** Remove the pancakes from the pan and let them cool completely on a wire rack.
9. **Assemble Dorayaki:** Once cooled, spread a generous amount of sweet red bean paste (anko) onto one pancake, then top with another pancake to form a sandwich.
10. **Serve:** Dorayaki can be served immediately or stored in an airtight container at room temperature for up to 2 days. Enjoy your homemade Dorayaki!

Dorayaki is loved for its soft, fluffy texture and sweet red bean filling, making it a delightful treat for any occasion.

Japanese Cotton Soft Cheesecake

Ingredients:

- 140g cream cheese, softened
- 50g unsalted butter
- 100ml milk
- 6 large eggs, separated
- 1/4 teaspoon cream of tartar
- 100g granulated sugar
- 1 tablespoon lemon juice
- 60g cake flour
- 20g cornstarch
- 1/4 teaspoon salt
- Powdered sugar, for dusting

Instructions:

1. **Preparation:** Preheat your oven to 320°F (160°C). Grease and line the bottom and sides of an 8-inch round cake pan with parchment paper.
2. **Melt Cream Cheese and Butter:** In a heatproof bowl, melt the cream cheese, butter, and milk together over a double boiler or in short bursts in the microwave until smooth. Set aside to cool slightly.
3. **Separate Eggs:** Separate the eggs into yolks and whites. Place the egg whites in a large mixing bowl and the yolks in a separate bowl.
4. **Whisk Egg Yolks:** Whisk the egg yolks with half of the granulated sugar until pale and creamy. Stir in the lemon juice.
5. **Combine Flour Mixture:** Sift together the cake flour, cornstarch, and salt. Gradually add this flour mixture to the egg yolk mixture, stirring until smooth.
6. **Mix Cheese Mixture:** Gradually add the cream cheese mixture to the egg yolk mixture, stirring until well combined and smooth.
7. **Beat Egg Whites:** Using a clean, dry mixer bowl, beat the egg whites with cream of tartar until foamy. Gradually add the remaining granulated sugar, a little at a time, while continuing to beat until stiff peaks form.
8. **Fold Egg Whites into Batter:** Gently fold the beaten egg whites into the cream cheese mixture in three batches, using a spatula. Be careful not to deflate the batter too much.
9. **Bake:** Pour the batter into the prepared cake pan and smooth the top with a spatula. Tap the pan gently on the counter to remove any air bubbles.
10. **Bake in Water Bath:** Place the cake pan into a larger baking dish. Fill the larger baking dish with hot water halfway up the sides of the cake pan (this helps create a moist baking environment).
11. **Bake in Oven:** Bake in the preheated oven for 70-80 minutes, or until the top is golden brown and the cake is set. The cake should jiggle slightly when gently shaken.
12. **Cooling:** Turn off the oven and leave the cake in the oven with the door slightly ajar for about 30 minutes to cool gradually. Remove the cake from the oven and let it cool completely in the cake pan on a wire rack.
13. **Dusting with Powdered Sugar:** Once cooled, dust the top of the cheesecake with powdered sugar.

14. **Serve:** Slice and serve your Japanese Cotton Soft Cheesecake, enjoying its light and fluffy texture.

This Japanese Cotton Soft Cheesecake is a delightful dessert that's perfect for any occasion, showcasing the delicate flavors and airy consistency that make it so beloved.

Hojicha (Roasted Green Tea) Cake

Ingredients:

- 1 cup all-purpose flour
- 1/2 cup hojicha powder (finely ground roasted green tea)
- 1 teaspoon baking powder
- 1/4 teaspoon baking soda
- 1/4 teaspoon salt
- 1/2 cup unsalted butter, softened
- 3/4 cup granulated sugar
- 2 large eggs
- 1 teaspoon vanilla extract
- 1/2 cup buttermilk (or 1/2 cup milk mixed with 1/2 tablespoon lemon juice or vinegar, let sit for 5 minutes)
- Whipped cream or frosting for topping (optional)

Instructions:

1. **Preparation:** Preheat your oven to 350°F (175°C). Grease and flour an 8-inch round cake pan or line it with parchment paper.
2. **Dry Ingredients:** In a bowl, whisk together the all-purpose flour, hojicha powder, baking powder, baking soda, and salt. Set aside.
3. **Cream Butter and Sugar:** In a large mixing bowl, cream together the softened butter and granulated sugar until light and fluffy.
4. **Add Eggs and Vanilla:** Add the eggs one at a time, mixing well after each addition. Stir in the vanilla extract.
5. **Combine Mixtures:** Gradually add the dry ingredients to the wet ingredients, alternating with buttermilk, beginning and ending with the flour mixture. Mix until just combined, being careful not to overmix.
6. **Bake:** Pour the batter into the prepared cake pan and spread it evenly.
7. **Bake:** Bake in the preheated oven for 25-30 minutes, or until a toothpick inserted into the center of the cake comes out clean.
8. **Cooling:** Remove the cake from the oven and let it cool in the pan for 10 minutes. Then, transfer the cake onto a wire rack to cool completely.
9. **Optional Topping:** Once cooled, you can top the Hojicha Cake with whipped cream or your favorite frosting for added flavor and decoration.
10. **Serve:** Slice and serve your Hojicha Cake, enjoying its unique roasted green tea flavor.

Hojicha Cake offers a delightful twist with its distinctive hojicha flavor, making it a perfect choice for tea lovers and those looking to explore Japanese-inspired desserts.

Uji Matcha Roll Cake

Ingredients:

For the Matcha Sponge Cake:

- 4 large eggs, separated
- 1/2 cup granulated sugar, divided
- 1/4 cup whole milk
- 1 tablespoon Uji matcha powder (high-quality matcha powder)
- 1/2 cup cake flour
- 1/4 teaspoon baking powder
- 1/4 teaspoon salt

For the Filling:

- 1 cup heavy cream, chilled
- 2-3 tablespoons powdered sugar (adjust to taste)
- 1 teaspoon vanilla extract

Optional:

- Extra matcha powder for dusting
- Fresh berries for garnish

Instructions:

1. Preheat and Prepare:

- Preheat your oven to 350°F (175°C). Line a 10x15-inch jelly roll pan with parchment paper, leaving some overhang for easy removal later.

2. Prepare the Matcha Sponge Cake:

- In a small bowl, whisk together the cake flour, matcha powder, baking powder, and salt. Set aside.
- In a large mixing bowl, beat the egg yolks and 1/4 cup of granulated sugar until pale and fluffy. Stir in the milk until well combined.
- Gradually fold the flour mixture into the egg yolk mixture until smooth.

3. Whip the Egg Whites:

- In a separate clean mixing bowl, beat the egg whites until frothy. Gradually add the remaining 1/4 cup of granulated sugar, continuing to beat until stiff peaks form.

4. Combine Mixtures:

- Gently fold the whipped egg whites into the matcha batter in three additions, being careful not to deflate the mixture.

- Spread the batter evenly into the prepared jelly roll pan, smoothing the top with a spatula.

5. Bake the Cake:

- Bake in the preheated oven for 12-15 minutes, or until the top of the cake springs back when lightly touched.

6. Roll the Cake:

- Remove the cake from the oven and immediately lift it out of the pan using the parchment paper overhang. Place it on a clean kitchen towel dusted with powdered sugar.
- Starting from one short end, gently roll the cake and towel together into a log. Let it cool completely on a wire rack.

7. Prepare the Filling:

- In a chilled mixing bowl, whip the heavy cream, powdered sugar, and vanilla extract until stiff peaks form.

8. Assemble the Roll Cake:

- Carefully unroll the cooled cake and remove the towel. Spread the whipped cream evenly over the surface of the cake.
- Re-roll the cake tightly without the towel, using the parchment paper to help if needed.
- Wrap the roll cake in plastic wrap and refrigerate for at least 1 hour to set.

9. Serve:

- Before serving, dust the Uji Matcha Roll Cake with additional matcha powder if desired. Garnish with fresh berries if desired.
- Slice and serve the roll cake chilled. Enjoy its delicate matcha flavor and light texture!

This Uji Matcha Roll Cake is a delightful dessert that beautifully showcases the unique flavor of Uji matcha, perfect for special occasions or as a treat for green tea enthusiasts.

Melon Pan Cake

Ingredients:

For the Cake Batter:

- 4 large eggs, separated
- 1/2 cup granulated sugar
- 1/4 cup whole milk
- 1/4 cup vegetable oil
- 1 teaspoon vanilla extract
- 1 cup cake flour
- 1 teaspoon baking powder
- 1/4 teaspoon salt

For the Cookie Crust:

- 1/2 cup unsalted butter, softened
- 1/2 cup granulated sugar
- 1 large egg
- 1 1/2 cups all-purpose flour
- 1/2 teaspoon baking powder
- 1/4 teaspoon salt
- Green food coloring (optional, for coloring the cookie crust)

Optional:

- Confectioners' sugar for dusting

Instructions:

1. Preheat and Prepare:

- Preheat your oven to 350°F (175°C). Grease and line a 9-inch round cake pan with parchment paper.

2. Prepare the Cake Batter:

- In a large mixing bowl, beat the egg yolks and granulated sugar until pale and fluffy.
- Stir in the milk, vegetable oil, and vanilla extract until well combined.
- In a separate bowl, sift together the cake flour, baking powder, and salt.
- Gradually add the dry ingredients to the wet ingredients, mixing until smooth and well combined.

3. Whip the Egg Whites:

- In another clean mixing bowl, beat the egg whites until frothy. Gradually add a tablespoon of granulated sugar at a time, continuing to beat until stiff peaks form.

4. Fold and Combine:

- Gently fold the whipped egg whites into the cake batter in three additions, being careful not to deflate the mixture.
- Pour the batter into the prepared cake pan and spread it evenly.

5. Prepare the Cookie Crust:

- In a separate bowl, cream together the softened butter and granulated sugar until light and fluffy.
- Beat in the egg until well combined.
- In another bowl, sift together the all-purpose flour, baking powder, and salt.
- Gradually add the dry ingredients to the butter mixture, mixing until a dough forms.
- Optionally, add a few drops of green food coloring to the cookie dough and mix until evenly colored.

6. Assemble and Bake:

- Divide the cookie dough into small pieces and flatten them to cover the top of the cake batter in the pan, forming a patchwork pattern (similar to melon pan).
- Bake in the preheated oven for 30-35 minutes, or until a toothpick inserted into the center comes out clean and the cookie crust is golden brown.

7. Cool and Serve:

- Remove the cake from the oven and let it cool in the pan for 10 minutes. Then, transfer the cake onto a wire rack to cool completely.
- Once cooled, dust the top of the Melon Pan Cake with confectioners' sugar if desired.
- Slice and serve the cake, enjoying the combination of fluffy cake with a sweet cookie crust reminiscent of melon pan.

This Melon Pan Cake combines the best of both worlds, offering a unique and delicious dessert that's sure to impress!

Japanese Strawberry Shortcake

Ingredients:

For the Sponge Cake:

- 4 large eggs
- 1/2 cup granulated sugar
- 1 teaspoon vanilla extract
- 1 cup cake flour (or 3/4 cup all-purpose flour + 1/4 cup cornstarch)
- 1 teaspoon baking powder
- 1/4 cup unsalted butter, melted and cooled

For the Filling and Decoration:

- 2 cups heavy cream, chilled
- 1/4 cup powdered sugar (adjust to taste)
- 1 teaspoon vanilla extract
- 1 pound fresh strawberries, washed, hulled, and sliced
- Additional whole strawberries for decoration

Optional:

- Strawberry jam or syrup (for brushing on cake layers)

Instructions:

1. Preheat and Prepare:

- Preheat your oven to 350°F (175°C). Grease and line two 8-inch round cake pans with parchment paper.

2. Prepare the Sponge Cake:

- In a large mixing bowl, beat the eggs, granulated sugar, and vanilla extract until pale and fluffy.
- Sift together the cake flour and baking powder. Gradually fold the flour mixture into the egg mixture until smooth.
- Fold in the melted butter gently until fully incorporated.
- Divide the batter evenly between the prepared cake pans and smooth the tops with a spatula.

3. Bake the Cake:

- Bake in the preheated oven for 20-25 minutes, or until the cakes are golden brown and a toothpick inserted into the center comes out clean.
- Remove from the oven and let the cakes cool in the pans for 10 minutes. Then, transfer them onto a wire rack to cool completely.

4. Prepare the Whipped Cream Filling:

- In a chilled mixing bowl, whip the heavy cream, powdered sugar, and vanilla extract until stiff peaks form.

5. Assemble the Cake:

- If desired, brush each cake layer with strawberry jam or syrup to add extra flavor.
- Place one cake layer on a serving plate. Spread a layer of whipped cream evenly over the top.
- Arrange a layer of sliced strawberries over the whipped cream.
- Place the second cake layer on top and gently press down.
- Frost the top and sides of the cake with the remaining whipped cream.
- Decorate the top of the cake with whole strawberries or additional sliced strawberries as desired.

6. Chill and Serve:

- Refrigerate the cake for at least 1 hour before serving to allow the flavors to meld and the whipped cream to set.
- Slice and serve your Japanese Strawberry Shortcake, enjoying the light and airy sponge layers with the fresh sweetness of strawberries and cream.

This Japanese Strawberry Shortcake is a beautiful and delicious dessert that's perfect for celebrations or any special occasion, showcasing the freshness of seasonal strawberries and the elegance of Japanese pastry techniques.

Satsuma Imo (Japanese Sweet Potato) Cake

Ingredients:

For the Cake:

- 1 cup mashed satsuma imo (Japanese sweet potato), cooled
- 1/2 cup unsalted butter, softened
- 1 cup granulated sugar
- 2 large eggs
- 1 teaspoon vanilla extract
- 1 1/2 cups all-purpose flour
- 1 1/2 teaspoons baking powder
- 1/4 teaspoon baking soda
- 1/4 teaspoon salt
- 1/2 cup buttermilk (or 1/2 cup milk mixed with 1/2 tablespoon lemon juice or vinegar, let sit for 5 minutes)

For the Frosting (optional):

- 4 oz cream cheese, softened
- 1/4 cup unsalted butter, softened
- 1 cup powdered sugar
- 1/2 teaspoon vanilla extract

Optional Garnish:

- Chopped toasted pecans or walnuts
- Cinnamon or nutmeg for dusting

Instructions:

1. Preheat and Prepare:

- Preheat your oven to 350°F (175°C). Grease and flour a 9-inch round cake pan or line it with parchment paper.

2. Prepare the Sweet Potato:

- Cook the satsuma imo (Japanese sweet potato) until tender. Mash and let it cool completely before using in the cake batter.

3. Make the Cake Batter:

- In a large mixing bowl, cream together the softened butter and granulated sugar until light and fluffy.
- Add the eggs one at a time, beating well after each addition. Stir in the vanilla extract.
- In a separate bowl, sift together the flour, baking powder, baking soda, and salt.

- Gradually add the dry ingredients to the butter mixture, alternating with buttermilk, beginning and ending with the flour mixture. Mix until just combined.
- Fold in the mashed satsuma imo until evenly distributed.

4. Bake the Cake:

- Pour the batter into the prepared cake pan and spread it evenly.
- Bake in the preheated oven for 25-30 minutes, or until a toothpick inserted into the center comes out clean.
- Remove from the oven and let the cake cool in the pan for 10 minutes. Then, transfer it onto a wire rack to cool completely.

5. Make the Frosting (optional):

- In a mixing bowl, beat the softened cream cheese and butter until smooth and creamy.
- Gradually add the powdered sugar and vanilla extract, beating until well combined and smooth.

6. Frost and Garnish (optional):

- Once the cake has cooled completely, frost the top and sides with the cream cheese frosting, if desired.
- Sprinkle chopped toasted pecans or walnuts on top, and dust with cinnamon or nutmeg for added flavor and decoration.

7. Serve and Enjoy:

- Slice and serve your Satsuma Imo Cake, enjoying the delicious combination of sweet potato flavor and moist cake texture.

This Satsuma Imo (Japanese Sweet Potato) Cake is a wonderful dessert that highlights the unique taste of satsuma imo, making it perfect for any occasion or as a special treat with a cup of tea or coffee.

Wagashi-inspired Cake

Wagashi-Inspired Cake Concept:

Cake Base:

- **Matcha Sponge Cake:** Use a light and fluffy matcha-flavored sponge cake as the base. Matcha adds a distinct Japanese flavor and vibrant green color.

Filling and Layers:

- **Red Bean Paste (Anko):** Include layers of sweet red bean paste (anko) between the cake layers. Anko is a common ingredient in Wagashi and adds a sweet, earthy flavor.

Decoration:

- **Sakura Blossoms:** Decorate the top of the cake with delicate Sakura blossoms made from fondant or edible rice paper. Sakura (cherry blossoms) are a symbol of spring in Japan and are often featured in Wagashi.
- **Gold Leaf or Powder:** Adorn the cake with edible gold leaf or gold powder for a touch of elegance, reflecting the refined aesthetic often found in traditional Japanese sweets.

Optional Components:

- **Yuzu Citrus Flavored Cream:** Incorporate a light yuzu citrus-flavored whipped cream between the layers for a refreshing contrast to the sweetness of the red bean paste.
- **Mochi Balls:** Include small mochi balls (rice cakes) as decorative elements around the base of the cake or on top. Mochi is another staple in Japanese confectionery.

Recipe: Matcha Sponge Cake

Ingredients:

- 4 large eggs, separated
- 1/2 cup granulated sugar
- 1 teaspoon vanilla extract
- 1/4 cup whole milk
- 1 tablespoon matcha powder
- 1 cup cake flour
- 1 teaspoon baking powder
- 1/4 teaspoon salt

Instructions:

1. **Preheat and Prepare:** Preheat your oven to 350°F (175°C). Grease and line two 8-inch round cake pans with parchment paper.
2. **Mix Dry Ingredients:** In a bowl, sift together the cake flour, matcha powder, baking powder, and salt. Set aside.

3. **Beat Egg Yolks:** In a large mixing bowl, beat the egg yolks and granulated sugar until thick and pale yellow. Add the vanilla extract and milk, and mix until combined.
4. **Fold in Dry Ingredients:** Gradually fold the dry ingredients into the egg yolk mixture until just combined. Be gentle to maintain the airiness of the batter.
5. **Whip Egg Whites:** In another clean mixing bowl, beat the egg whites until stiff peaks form.
6. **Combine Batter:** Gently fold the whipped egg whites into the batter in three additions, incorporating fully but gently to keep the batter light.
7. **Bake:** Divide the batter evenly between the prepared cake pans. Smooth the tops with a spatula. Bake for 20-25 minutes, or until a toothpick inserted into the center comes out clean.
8. **Cool and Assemble:** Let the cakes cool in the pans for 10 minutes, then transfer to a wire rack to cool completely.
9. **Assemble the Cake:** Once cooled, place one cake layer on a serving plate. Spread a layer of sweetened red bean paste (anko) on top. Add a layer of yuzu-flavored whipped cream, if using. Place the second cake layer on top.
10. **Decorate:** Frost the top and sides of the cake with more yuzu-flavored whipped cream. Decorate with Sakura blossoms made from fondant or edible rice paper. Add small mochi balls around the base or on top. Dust with gold leaf or gold powder for a luxurious finish.
11. **Serve:** Slice and serve your Wagashi-inspired cake, enjoying the harmonious blend of traditional Japanese flavors and modern cake design.

This Wagashi-inspired cake combines traditional Japanese confectionery elements with a contemporary cake structure, perfect for special occasions or for celebrating Japanese culture through dessert.

Shingen Mochi Cake

Ingredients:

For the Cake:

- 1 cup all-purpose flour
- 1/2 cup kinako (roasted soybean flour)
- 1/2 cup granulated sugar
- 1 teaspoon baking powder
- 1/2 teaspoon baking soda
- 1/4 teaspoon salt
- 1/2 cup unsalted butter, softened
- 2 large eggs
- 1 teaspoon vanilla extract
- 1 cup buttermilk (or 1 cup milk + 1 tablespoon lemon juice, let sit for 5 minutes)

For the Syrup:

- 1/2 cup kuromitsu (Japanese brown sugar syrup)
- 1/4 cup water

For Garnish (optional):

- Additional kinako for dusting
- Edible gold leaf or gold powder

Instructions:

1. Preheat and Prepare:

- Preheat your oven to 350°F (175°C). Grease and flour an 8-inch round cake pan or line it with parchment paper.

2. Mix Dry Ingredients:

- In a bowl, sift together the all-purpose flour, kinako, baking powder, baking soda, and salt. Set aside.

3. Cream Butter and Sugar:

- In a large mixing bowl, cream together the softened butter and granulated sugar until light and fluffy.

4. Add Eggs and Vanilla:

- Beat in the eggs, one at a time, ensuring each is fully incorporated before adding the next. Stir in the vanilla extract.

5. Combine Wet and Dry Ingredients:

- Gradually add the dry ingredients to the butter mixture, alternating with buttermilk, beginning and ending with the flour mixture. Mix until just combined.

6. Bake the Cake:

- Pour the batter into the prepared cake pan and smooth the top with a spatula.
- Bake in the preheated oven for 25-30 minutes, or until a toothpick inserted into the center comes out clean.
- Remove from the oven and let the cake cool in the pan for 10 minutes. Then, transfer it onto a wire rack to cool completely.

7. Prepare the Syrup:

- In a small saucepan, combine the kuromitsu and water. Heat over medium heat until the mixture is well combined and slightly thickened, about 5 minutes. Remove from heat and let it cool slightly.

8. Assemble the Cake:

- Once the cake has cooled, place it on a serving plate. Poke several holes in the top of the cake using a skewer or fork.
- Pour the kuromitsu syrup evenly over the top of the cake, allowing it to soak into the cake.

9. Garnish (optional):

- Dust the top of the cake with additional kinako for added flavor and texture.
- Optionally, decorate with edible gold leaf or gold powder for a touch of elegance.

10. Serve:

- Slice and serve your Shingen Mochi Cake, enjoying the unique combination of kinako and kuromitsu flavors reminiscent of traditional Japanese sweets.

This Shingen Mochi Cake offers a modern twist on a classic Japanese treat, perfect for sharing with friends and family while celebrating the flavors of Japan.

Mitarashi Dango (Skewered Rice Dumplings) Cake

Cake Base:

Rice Flour Cake:

- Create a light and fluffy rice flour-based cake that mimics the texture of dango. This cake base will serve as the foundation for the Mitarashi Dango flavors.

Filling and Layers:

Sweet Soy Sauce Glaze:

- Incorporate a sweet soy sauce glaze into the layers of the cake to infuse it with the characteristic flavor of Mitarashi Dango.

Decoration:

Dango Skewers:

- Decorate the top of the cake with miniature dango skewers made from rice flour balls, resembling traditional Mitarashi Dango presentation.

Optional Components:

Kinako (Roasted Soybean Flour):

- Sprinkle kinako over the cake layers or as a garnish on top for added flavor and texture.

Black Sesame Seeds:

- Garnish the cake with black sesame seeds for a contrast in color and a nutty flavor profile.

Recipe: Rice Flour Cake with Mitarashi Dango Flavors

Ingredients:

For the Cake:

- 1 cup rice flour
- 1 cup all-purpose flour
- 1 teaspoon baking powder
- 1/2 teaspoon baking soda
- 1/4 teaspoon salt
- 1/2 cup unsalted butter, softened
- 1 cup granulated sugar
- 2 large eggs
- 1 cup buttermilk (or 1 cup milk + 1 tablespoon lemon juice, let sit for 5 minutes)
- 1 teaspoon vanilla extract

For the Sweet Soy Sauce Glaze:

- 1/2 cup soy sauce
- 1/2 cup mirin (Japanese sweet rice wine)
- 1/4 cup granulated sugar
- 2 tablespoons cornstarch
- 1/4 cup water

For Garnish:

- Miniature dango skewers (made from small rice flour balls)
- Kinako (roasted soybean flour)
- Black sesame seeds

Instructions:

1. Preheat and Prepare:

- Preheat your oven to 350°F (175°C). Grease and flour a 9-inch round cake pan or line it with parchment paper.

2. Mix Dry Ingredients:

- In a bowl, sift together the rice flour, all-purpose flour, baking powder, baking soda, and salt. Set aside.

3. Cream Butter and Sugar:

- In a large mixing bowl, cream together the softened butter and granulated sugar until light and fluffy.

4. Add Eggs and Vanilla:

- Beat in the eggs, one at a time, ensuring each is fully incorporated before adding the next. Stir in the vanilla extract.

5. Combine Wet and Dry Ingredients:

- Gradually add the dry ingredients to the butter mixture, alternating with buttermilk, beginning and ending with the flour mixture. Mix until just combined.

6. Bake the Cake:

- Pour the batter into the prepared cake pan and smooth the top with a spatula.
- Bake in the preheated oven for 25-30 minutes, or until a toothpick inserted into the center comes out clean.
- Remove from the oven and let the cake cool in the pan for 10 minutes. Then, transfer it onto a wire rack to cool completely.

7. Prepare the Sweet Soy Sauce Glaze:

- In a small saucepan, combine the soy sauce, mirin, and granulated sugar. Bring to a boil over medium heat, stirring until the sugar is dissolved.
- In a separate bowl, mix the cornstarch and water until smooth. Gradually whisk the cornstarch mixture into the soy sauce mixture.
- Continue to cook, stirring constantly, until the glaze thickens. Remove from heat and let it cool slightly.

8. Assemble the Cake:

- Once the cake has cooled, place it on a serving plate. Pierce the top of the cake with a skewer or fork to allow the glaze to penetrate.
- Pour the sweet soy sauce glaze evenly over the top of the cake, allowing it to soak in and drizzle down the sides.

9. Garnish and Serve:

- Arrange miniature dango skewers on top of the cake, using toothpicks or small skewers to hold them in place.
- Sprinkle kinako and black sesame seeds over the top for additional flavor and decoration.
- Slice and serve your Mitarashi Dango Cake, enjoying the unique fusion of traditional Japanese flavors with a modern cake presentation.

This Mitarashi Dango-inspired cake offers a creative twist on a beloved Japanese dessert, combining the essence of Mitarashi Dango with the texture and structure of a cake for a delightful and memorable dessert experience.

Wasabi Cake

Cake Base:

Vanilla or White Chocolate Cake:

- Use a light and moist vanilla or white chocolate cake base to provide a neutral backdrop for the bold flavor of wasabi.

Filling and Layers:

Wasabi Buttercream:

- Create a creamy and smooth buttercream frosting infused with wasabi paste. Adjust the amount of wasabi to achieve the desired level of spiciness.

Decoration:

Garnish with Pistachios and Dark Chocolate:

- Garnish the cake with crushed pistachios and shavings of dark chocolate to complement and balance the spiciness of the wasabi.

Optional Components:

Citrus Zest or Lemon Curd:

- Incorporate citrus zest or lemon curd between the cake layers to add a refreshing contrast to the heat of the wasabi.

Recipe: Wasabi Cake with Pistachios and Dark Chocolate

Ingredients:

For the Cake:

- 1 3/4 cups all-purpose flour
- 1 1/2 teaspoons baking powder
- 1/2 teaspoon baking soda
- 1/4 teaspoon salt
- 1/2 cup unsalted butter, softened
- 1 cup granulated sugar
- 2 large eggs
- 1 teaspoon vanilla extract
- 3/4 cup buttermilk (or 3/4 cup milk + 3/4 tablespoon lemon juice, let sit for 5 minutes)

For the Wasabi Buttercream:

- 1 cup unsalted butter, softened

- 3-4 cups powdered sugar, sifted
- 1-2 tablespoons wasabi paste (adjust to taste)
- 1-2 tablespoons heavy cream or milk (if needed)
- Green food coloring (optional, for color)

For Decoration:

- Crushed pistachios, for garnish
- Dark chocolate shavings or curls, for garnish

Instructions:

1. Preheat and Prepare:

- Preheat your oven to 350°F (175°C). Grease and flour two 8-inch round cake pans or line them with parchment paper.

2. Mix Dry Ingredients:

- In a bowl, sift together the flour, baking powder, baking soda, and salt. Set aside.

3. Cream Butter and Sugar:

- In a large mixing bowl, cream together the softened butter and granulated sugar until light and fluffy.

4. Add Eggs and Vanilla:

- Beat in the eggs, one at a time, ensuring each is fully incorporated before adding the next. Stir in the vanilla extract.

5. Combine Wet and Dry Ingredients:

- Gradually add the dry ingredients to the butter mixture, alternating with buttermilk, beginning and ending with the flour mixture. Mix until just combined.

6. Bake the Cake:

- Divide the batter evenly between the prepared cake pans. Smooth the tops with a spatula.
- Bake in the preheated oven for 25-30 minutes, or until a toothpick inserted into the center comes out clean.
- Remove from the oven and let the cakes cool in the pans for 10 minutes. Then, transfer them onto a wire rack to cool completely.

7. Make the Wasabi Buttercream:

- In a mixing bowl, beat the softened butter until smooth and creamy.
- Gradually add the powdered sugar, 1 cup at a time, beating well after each addition until smooth.

- Mix in the wasabi paste to taste, adjusting the amount for desired spiciness. If the buttercream is too thick, add heavy cream or milk, a tablespoon at a time, until desired consistency is reached. Optionally, add green food coloring for a vibrant look.

8. Assemble the Cake:

- Once the cakes are completely cooled, place one cake layer on a serving plate or cake stand.
- Spread a layer of wasabi buttercream evenly over the top.
- Place the second cake layer on top and frost the top and sides of the cake with the remaining buttercream.

9. Decorate the Cake:

- Press crushed pistachios onto the sides of the cake for texture and flavor.
- Sprinkle dark chocolate shavings or curls over the top for additional decoration.

10. Serve:

- Slice and serve your Wasabi Cake, enjoying the unique blend of spicy wasabi with the sweetness of the cake and the crunch of pistachios and dark chocolate.

This Wasabi Cake recipe offers a bold and unexpected twist on traditional cakes, incorporating the distinctive flavor of wasabi into a dessert that's sure to intrigue and delight adventurous taste buds. Adjust the amount of wasabi according to your preference for spiciness, ensuring a harmonious balance with the other flavors and textures.

Yomogi (Japanese Mugwort) Cake

Cake Base:

Yomogi Sponge Cake:

- Make a light and fluffy sponge cake infused with yomogi paste or finely chopped yomogi leaves. This will give the cake a green hue and a subtle herbal flavor.

Filling and Layers:

Sweet Red Bean Paste (Anko):

- Use layers of sweet red bean paste (anko) between the cake layers. Anko complements the herbal notes of yomogi and adds sweetness.

Decoration:

Whipped Cream or Frosting:

- Frost the cake with whipped cream or a light frosting to balance the flavors and textures. Optionally, decorate with yomogi leaves or edible flowers for a touch of elegance.

Optional Components:

Yuzu Citrus Curd:

- Include a layer of yuzu citrus curd between the cake layers for a refreshing and tangy contrast.

Recipe: Yomogi (Japanese Mugwort) Cake

Ingredients:

For the Yomogi Sponge Cake:

- 4 large eggs, separated
- 1/2 cup granulated sugar
- 1/2 cup yomogi paste or finely chopped yomogi leaves
- 1 cup cake flour
- 1 teaspoon baking powder
- 1/4 teaspoon salt

For the Filling:

- 1 cup sweet red bean paste (anko)

For the Frosting:

- 2 cups heavy cream

- 1/4 cup powdered sugar
- 1 teaspoon vanilla extract

Optional:

- Yuzu citrus curd (store-bought or homemade) for filling
- Yomogi leaves or edible flowers for decoration

Instructions:

1. Preheat and Prepare:

- Preheat your oven to 350°F (175°C). Grease and line two 8-inch round cake pans with parchment paper.

2. Make Yomogi Paste (if using fresh yomogi leaves):

- Blanch the yomogi leaves briefly in boiling water, then shock in ice water to retain their vibrant green color. Drain and squeeze out excess water.
- Blend the blanched yomogi leaves with a little water until smooth to create a yomogi paste.

3. Mix Dry Ingredients:

- In a bowl, sift together the cake flour, baking powder, and salt. Set aside.

4. Prepare Yomogi Sponge Cake:

- In a large mixing bowl, beat the egg yolks and granulated sugar until pale and creamy.
- Mix in the yomogi paste (or finely chopped yomogi leaves) until well combined.
- Gradually add the sifted dry ingredients to the yolk mixture, mixing until smooth.

5. Whip Egg Whites:

- In a separate bowl, beat the egg whites until stiff peaks form.

6. Combine Batter:

- Gently fold the whipped egg whites into the yomogi batter in three additions, folding until just combined. Be careful not to deflate the batter.

7. Bake the Cake:

- Divide the batter evenly between the prepared cake pans. Smooth the tops with a spatula.
- Bake in the preheated oven for 20-25 minutes, or until a toothpick inserted into the center comes out clean.
- Remove from the oven and let the cakes cool in the pans for 10 minutes. Then, transfer them onto a wire rack to cool completely.

8. Make Whipped Cream Frosting:

- In a chilled mixing bowl, whip the heavy cream until soft peaks form.
- Gradually add the powdered sugar and vanilla extract, continuing to whip until stiff peaks form.

9. Assemble the Cake:

- Once the cakes are completely cooled, place one cake layer on a serving plate or cake stand.
- Spread a layer of sweet red bean paste (anko) evenly over the cake layer.
- Optionally, spread yuzu citrus curd over the anko layer for added flavor.
- Place the second cake layer on top and frost the top and sides of the cake with the whipped cream frosting.

10. Decorate:

- Garnish the cake with yomogi leaves or edible flowers for a decorative touch.

11. Serve:

- Slice and serve your Yomogi Cake, enjoying the delicate herbal flavor of yomogi paired with sweet red bean paste and fluffy whipped cream.

This Yomogi Cake recipe captures the essence of Japanese cuisine with its unique use of yomogi and anko, creating a dessert that's both delicious and visually appealing. Adjust the sweetness and filling according to your preference, ensuring a perfect balance of flavors in every bite.

Anmitsu Cake

Cake Base:

Vanilla Sponge Cake:

- Use a light and fluffy vanilla sponge cake as the base. This will provide a neutral backdrop to complement the flavors of the Anmitsu components.

Filling and Layers:

Agar Jelly Cubes:

- Incorporate agar jelly cubes flavored with matcha or fruit juice between the cake layers. Agar jelly adds texture and authenticity to the Anmitsu experience.

Sweet Red Bean Paste (Anko):

- Layer the cake with sweet red bean paste (anko), which is a staple in traditional Anmitsu and provides a rich, sweet contrast.

Fruits:

- Add a layer of fresh fruits such as strawberries, mandarin oranges, and kiwi. Choose fruits that complement the flavors of the Anmitsu components.

Decoration:

Mitsumame Syrup:

- Drizzle the cake layers with Mitsumame syrup, which is typically made from sugar syrup with agar jelly cubes and fruits.

Optional Components:

Whipped Cream:

- Use whipped cream between the layers for added lightness and creaminess.

Shiratama Dango (Rice Dumplings):

- Optionally include small shiratama dango (rice dumplings) as decorative elements on top of the cake.

Recipe: Anmitsu Cake

Ingredients:

For the Vanilla Sponge Cake:

- 1 3/4 cups all-purpose flour
- 1 1/2 teaspoons baking powder
- 1/2 teaspoon baking soda
- 1/4 teaspoon salt
- 1/2 cup unsalted butter, softened
- 1 cup granulated sugar
- 2 large eggs
- 1 teaspoon vanilla extract
- 3/4 cup buttermilk (or 3/4 cup milk + 3/4 tablespoon lemon juice, let sit for 5 minutes)

For the Agar Jelly Cubes:

- 2 cups water
- 1/4 cup agar agar powder
- 1/4 cup granulated sugar
- Flavored extract or juice (optional, for coloring and flavor)

For the Assembly:

- 1 cup sweet red bean paste (anko)
- Assorted fresh fruits (e.g., strawberries, mandarin oranges, kiwi)
- Mitsumame syrup (sugar syrup with agar jelly cubes and fruits)
- Whipped cream (optional)
- Shiratama dango (optional, for decoration)

Instructions:

1. Preheat and Prepare:

- Preheat your oven to 350°F (175°C). Grease and flour two 8-inch round cake pans or line them with parchment paper.

2. Make the Vanilla Sponge Cake:

- In a bowl, sift together the flour, baking powder, baking soda, and salt. Set aside.
- In a large mixing bowl, cream together the softened butter and granulated sugar until light and fluffy.
- Beat in the eggs, one at a time, ensuring each is fully incorporated before adding the next. Stir in the vanilla extract.
- Gradually add the dry ingredients to the butter mixture, alternating with buttermilk, beginning and ending with the flour mixture. Mix until just combined.
- Divide the batter evenly between the prepared cake pans. Smooth the tops with a spatula.
- Bake in the preheated oven for 20-25 minutes, or until a toothpick inserted into the center comes out clean.
- Remove from the oven and let the cakes cool in the pans for 10 minutes. Then, transfer them onto a wire rack to cool completely.

3. Make the Agar Jelly Cubes:

- In a saucepan, bring the water to a boil. Reduce the heat and whisk in the agar agar powder and sugar until dissolved.
- If desired, add a few drops of flavored extract or juice for coloring and flavor.
- Pour the mixture into a shallow pan or dish and let it set at room temperature until firm. Once set, cut into small cubes.

4. Assemble the Anmitsu Cake:

- Place one cooled cake layer on a serving plate or cake stand.
- Spread a layer of sweet red bean paste (anko) evenly over the cake layer.
- Arrange a layer of assorted fresh fruits (sliced or whole, as desired) over the anko layer.
- Scatter the agar jelly cubes over the fruits.
- Optionally, drizzle Mitsumame syrup over the fruit and jelly layer.
- Place the second cake layer on top and repeat the filling layers (anko, fruits, agar jelly cubes, Mitsumame syrup).

5. Optional Decoration:

- Frost the top and sides of the cake with whipped cream, if desired.
- Garnish with additional fresh fruits, agar jelly cubes, and shiratama dango (rice dumplings).

6. Serve:

- Slice and serve your Anmitsu Cake, enjoying the delightful combination of flavors and textures reminiscent of traditional Japanese Anmitsu dessert.

This Anmitsu Cake recipe offers a creative twist on a beloved Japanese dessert, combining the essence of Anmitsu with the structure and presentation of a layered cake, perfect for special occasions or celebrations. Adjust the components and decorations according to your taste preferences for a personalized touch.

Chestnut Cake

Cake Base:

Chestnut Flour Cake:

- Use chestnut flour as the primary ingredient to infuse the cake with a deep, nutty flavor. Chestnut flour adds a unique texture and richness to the cake.

Filling and Layers:

Chestnut Puree Filling:

- Incorporate a creamy chestnut puree filling between the cake layers. Chestnut puree complements the chestnut flour cake and enhances its flavor profile.

Whipped Cream or Buttercream Frosting:

- Use a light and fluffy whipped cream or buttercream frosting between the layers to add sweetness and balance to the nutty flavors.

Decoration:

Candied Chestnuts:

- Garnish the cake with candied chestnuts or chopped roasted chestnuts for texture and visual appeal.

Optional Components:

Rum or Brandy Syrup:

- Optionally, soak the cake layers with a rum or brandy syrup to enhance the flavor and keep the cake moist.

Chocolate Ganache:

- Drizzle chocolate ganache over the top of the cake or between layers for added richness and contrast.

Recipe: Chestnut Cake

Ingredients:

For the Chestnut Cake:

- 1 1/2 cups chestnut flour
- 1 cup all-purpose flour
- 2 teaspoons baking powder

- 1/2 teaspoon baking soda
- 1/2 teaspoon salt
- 1 cup unsalted butter, softened
- 1 cup granulated sugar
- 4 large eggs
- 1 teaspoon vanilla extract
- 1 cup buttermilk (or 1 cup milk + 1 tablespoon lemon juice, let sit for 5 minutes)

For the Chestnut Puree Filling:

- 1 cup sweetened chestnut puree (available in jars or cans)
- 1/2 cup heavy cream, whipped (optional, for lightening the texture)

For the Frosting:

- 2 cups heavy cream, chilled
- 1/2 cup powdered sugar
- 1 teaspoon vanilla extract

For Decoration:

- Candied chestnuts or chopped roasted chestnuts
- Chocolate ganache (optional, for drizzling)

Instructions:

1. Preheat and Prepare:

- Preheat your oven to 350°F (175°C). Grease and flour two 8-inch round cake pans or line them with parchment paper.

2. Mix Dry Ingredients:

- In a bowl, sift together the chestnut flour, all-purpose flour, baking powder, baking soda, and salt. Set aside.

3. Cream Butter and Sugar:

- In a large mixing bowl, cream together the softened butter and granulated sugar until light and fluffy.

4. Add Eggs and Vanilla:

- Beat in the eggs, one at a time, ensuring each is fully incorporated before adding the next. Stir in the vanilla extract.

5. Combine Wet and Dry Ingredients:

- Gradually add the dry ingredients to the butter mixture, alternating with buttermilk, beginning and ending with the flour mixture. Mix until just combined.

6. Bake the Cake:

- Divide the batter evenly between the prepared cake pans. Smooth the tops with a spatula.
- Bake in the preheated oven for 25-30 minutes, or until a toothpick inserted into the center comes out clean.
- Remove from the oven and let the cakes cool in the pans for 10 minutes. Then, transfer them onto a wire rack to cool completely.

7. Make the Chestnut Puree Filling:

- If using unsweetened chestnut puree, sweeten it to taste with powdered sugar or honey.
- Optionally, fold in whipped cream to lighten the texture of the chestnut puree.

8. Make the Frosting:

- In a chilled mixing bowl, whip the heavy cream until soft peaks form.
- Gradually add the powdered sugar and vanilla extract, continuing to whip until stiff peaks form.

9. Assemble the Cake:

- Once the cakes are completely cooled, place one cake layer on a serving plate or cake stand.
- Spread the chestnut puree filling evenly over the cake layer.
- Place the second cake layer on top and frost the top and sides of the cake with the whipped cream frosting.

10. Decorate:

- Garnish the top of the cake with candied chestnuts or chopped roasted chestnuts.
- Optionally, drizzle chocolate ganache over the top or between layers for added decadence.

11. Serve:

- Slice and serve your Chestnut Cake, enjoying the rich, nutty flavors and creamy texture of the chestnut puree and whipped cream.

This Chestnut Cake recipe offers a luxurious dessert experience, perfect for showcasing the distinctive flavor of chestnuts in a beautifully layered cake. Adjust the sweetness and decorations according to your taste preferences for a delightful culinary treat.

Dorayaki-inspired Cake

Cake Base:

Buttermilk Pancake Cake Layers:

- Use fluffy buttermilk pancakes as the base for this cake. These pancakes will mimic the texture of Dorayaki pancakes.

Filling and Layers:

Sweet Red Bean Paste (Anko) Filling:

- Sandwich layers of sweet red bean paste (anko) between the pancake cake layers. Anko provides a rich and sweet contrast to the fluffy pancakes.

Decoration:

Honey Drizzle:

- Drizzle honey over the top layer and around the sides of the cake for added sweetness and gloss, reminiscent of Dorayaki.

Optional Components:

Whipped Cream:

- Optionally, layer the cake with whipped cream for added lightness and creaminess.

Matcha Powder Dusting:

- Dust the top of the cake with matcha powder for a touch of color and to complement the traditional Japanese flavors.

Recipe: Dorayaki-inspired Cake

Ingredients:

For the Buttermilk Pancake Cake Layers:

- 2 cups all-purpose flour
- 2 tablespoons granulated sugar
- 2 teaspoons baking powder
- 1/2 teaspoon baking soda
- 1/4 teaspoon salt
- 2 cups buttermilk
- 2 large eggs
- 4 tablespoons unsalted butter, melted and cooled
- 1 teaspoon vanilla extract

For the Filling:

- 1 cup sweet red bean paste (anko)

For Decoration:

- Honey, for drizzling
- Matcha powder, for dusting

Instructions:

1. Prepare Pancake Cake Layers:

- In a large mixing bowl, whisk together the flour, sugar, baking powder, baking soda, and salt.
- In another bowl, whisk together the buttermilk, eggs, melted butter, and vanilla extract.
- Pour the wet ingredients into the dry ingredients and stir until just combined. Do not overmix; a few lumps are okay.
- Heat a non-stick skillet or griddle over medium heat and lightly grease with butter or oil.
- Pour about 1/4 cup of batter onto the skillet for each pancake. Cook until bubbles form on the surface of the pancake and the edges look set, about 2-3 minutes. Flip and cook for another 1-2 minutes until golden brown.
- Transfer the cooked pancakes to a plate and repeat with the remaining batter. You should have about 8-10 pancakes depending on the size.

2. Assemble the Dorayaki-inspired Cake:

- Place one pancake on a serving plate or cake stand.
- Spread a layer of sweet red bean paste (anko) evenly over the pancake.
- Repeat with the remaining pancakes and anko, stacking them alternately.
- Once all pancakes and anko are layered, drizzle honey over the top layer and around the sides of the cake.
- Optionally, dust the top of the cake with matcha powder for decoration and flavor.
- Chill the cake in the refrigerator for about 30 minutes to allow the flavors to meld.

3. Serve:

- Slice and serve your Dorayaki-inspired Cake, enjoying the combination of fluffy pancakes with sweet red bean paste and a touch of honey.

Ichigo Daifuku (Strawberry Mochi) Cake

Cake Base:

Soft Mochi Layers:

- Create soft mochi layers that mimic the texture and sweetness of traditional daifuku mochi. These layers will envelop the sweet red bean paste (anko) and fresh strawberries.

Filling and Layers:

Sweet Red Bean Paste (Anko) and Strawberry Filling:

- Alternate layers of sweet red bean paste (anko) and sliced fresh strawberries between the mochi layers. This combination provides a balance of sweetness and freshness.

Decoration:

Powdered Sugar Dusting:

- Dust the top of the cake with powdered sugar for a traditional touch and added sweetness.

Optional Components:

Whipped Cream or Cream Cheese Frosting:

- Optionally, layer the cake with whipped cream or cream cheese frosting for added richness and creaminess.

Additional Strawberries:

- Garnish the top of the cake with whole strawberries or strawberry slices for a decorative and delicious finish.

Recipe: Ichigo Daifuku Cake

Ingredients:

For the Mochi Layers:

- 1 cup mochiko (sweet rice flour)
- 1/4 cup granulated sugar
- 1 cup water
- Potato starch or cornstarch, for dusting

For the Filling:

- 1 cup sweet red bean paste (anko)
- 1 pint fresh strawberries, hulled and sliced

Optional Frosting:

- 1 cup whipped cream or cream cheese frosting (store-bought or homemade)

For Decoration:

- Powdered sugar, for dusting
- Fresh strawberries, for garnish

Instructions:

1. Prepare Mochi Layers:

- In a microwave-safe bowl, whisk together the mochiko and sugar.
- Gradually stir in the water until smooth.
- Cover the bowl loosely with plastic wrap or a microwave-safe lid.
- Microwave on high for 2-3 minutes, stopping to stir every minute, until the mochi mixture is thick and sticky.
- Dust a clean work surface with potato starch or cornstarch.
- Transfer the hot mochi mixture onto the dusted surface and knead it with a spatula or your hands until smooth and elastic.
- Divide the mochi into 3 equal portions.
- Roll out each portion of mochi into a thin, even layer (about 1/4 inch thick) using a rolling pin dusted with potato starch or cornstarch.
- Use an 8-inch round cake pan or a cake ring as a guide to cut out 3 circles of mochi. Set aside to cool completely.

2. Assemble the Ichigo Daifuku Cake:

- Place one mochi circle on a serving plate or cake stand.
- Spread a layer of sweet red bean paste (anko) evenly over the mochi.
- Arrange a layer of sliced strawberries over the anko.
- Repeat with another layer of mochi, anko, and strawberries.
- Place the third mochi circle on top, finishing the layers.
- Optionally, frost the top and sides of the cake with whipped cream or cream cheese frosting.

3. Decoration and Serving:

- Dust the top of the cake with powdered sugar.
- Garnish with fresh strawberries on top of the cake for decoration.
- Chill the cake in the refrigerator for about 1 hour before slicing to allow the flavors to meld and the mochi to set.
- Slice and serve your Ichigo Daifuku Cake, enjoying the combination of soft mochi, sweet red bean paste, and fresh strawberries in every bite.

This Ichigo Daifuku Cake recipe offers a delightful twist on the classic Japanese sweet, transforming it into a layered cake format while preserving the essence of its traditional flavors and textures. Adjust the sweetness and decorations according to your taste preferences for a unique and delicious dessert experience.

Tofu Cheesecake

Crust:

Graham Cracker Crust:

- Use a classic graham cracker crust for a sweet and crunchy base that complements the creamy tofu filling.

Filling:

Tofu and Cream Cheese Blend:

- Blend silken tofu with cream cheese for a smooth and creamy filling. Tofu provides a lighter texture compared to traditional cheesecake while maintaining richness.

Flavoring:

Vanilla and Lemon Zest:

- Flavor the cheesecake with vanilla extract and lemon zest for a refreshing and citrusy twist.

Decoration:

Fresh Fruit or Fruit Compote:

- Top the cheesecake with fresh berries or a homemade fruit compote for added sweetness and color.

Optional Components:

Agar Agar for Vegan Option:

- Optionally, use agar agar to set the cheesecake instead of gelatin, making it suitable for vegans.

Recipe: Tofu Cheesecake

Ingredients:

For the Graham Cracker Crust:

- 1 1/2 cups graham cracker crumbs
- 1/4 cup granulated sugar
- 1/2 cup unsalted butter, melted

For the Tofu Cheesecake Filling:

- 1 pound silken tofu, drained
- 1 (8-ounce) package cream cheese, softened

- 1/2 cup granulated sugar
- 2 tablespoons cornstarch
- 1 teaspoon vanilla extract
- Zest of 1 lemon
- 2 tablespoons fresh lemon juice

For Decoration (Optional):

- Fresh berries or fruit compote

Instructions:

1. Preheat and Prepare:

- Preheat your oven to 350°F (175°C). Grease a 9-inch springform pan or line the bottom with parchment paper.

2. Make the Graham Cracker Crust:

- In a bowl, combine the graham cracker crumbs, sugar, and melted butter. Mix until the crumbs are evenly moistened.
- Press the mixture firmly into the bottom of the prepared pan to form an even crust.
- Bake the crust in the preheated oven for 8-10 minutes, until lightly golden. Remove from the oven and let it cool while preparing the filling.

3. Make the Tofu Cheesecake Filling:

- In a blender or food processor, blend the silken tofu until smooth and creamy.
- Add the softened cream cheese, granulated sugar, cornstarch, vanilla extract, lemon zest, and lemon juice. Blend until all ingredients are well combined and the mixture is smooth.

4. Assemble and Bake:

- Pour the tofu cheesecake filling over the cooled graham cracker crust in the springform pan.
- Smooth the top with a spatula to ensure an even layer.
- Bake the cheesecake in the preheated oven for 40-45 minutes, or until the edges are set and the center is slightly jiggly.
- Turn off the oven and leave the cheesecake inside with the door slightly ajar for about 30 minutes to cool gradually.

5. Chill and Serve:

- Remove the cheesecake from the oven and let it cool completely at room temperature.
- Refrigerate the cheesecake for at least 4 hours or overnight to set and chill.

6. Decoration (Optional):

- Before serving, top the chilled cheesecake with fresh berries or a fruit compote for decoration and added flavor.

7. Serve:

- Release the springform pan and transfer the tofu cheesecake to a serving platter.
- Slice and serve chilled. Enjoy the light and creamy texture of this Tofu Cheesecake with its refreshing lemon and vanilla flavors.

This Tofu Cheesecake recipe offers a healthier alternative to traditional cheesecake without compromising on taste or texture, making it a delightful dessert option for those looking for a lighter treat. Adjust the sweetness and flavorings according to your preference for a personalized touch.

Soba Cha (Buckwheat Tea) Cake

Cake Base:

Buckwheat Flour Cake:

- Use buckwheat flour as the primary ingredient to capture the distinctive flavor of soba cha. Buckwheat flour adds a nutty depth to the cake.

Flavoring:

Honey and Cinnamon:

- Enhance the flavor profile with honey for sweetness and cinnamon for warmth, complementing the nuttiness of buckwheat.

Decoration:

Powdered Sugar Dusting:

- Dust the top of the cake with powdered sugar for a simple and elegant finish.

Optional Components:

Whipped Cream or Cream Cheese Frosting:

- Optionally, frost the cake with whipped cream or cream cheese frosting for added richness and texture.

Nuts or Seeds:

- Sprinkle chopped nuts or seeds on top of the cake for added crunch and visual appeal.

Recipe: Soba Cha Cake

Ingredients:

For the Buckwheat Cake:

- 1 cup buckwheat flour
- 1 cup all-purpose flour
- 1 teaspoon baking powder
- 1/2 teaspoon baking soda
- 1/4 teaspoon salt
- 1/2 cup unsalted butter, softened
- 1/2 cup granulated sugar
- 1/2 cup honey
- 2 large eggs
- 1 cup buttermilk (or 1 cup milk + 1 tablespoon lemon juice, let sit for 5 minutes)

- 1 teaspoon vanilla extract
- 1 teaspoon ground cinnamon (optional, for flavor enhancement)

For Decoration:

- Powdered sugar, for dusting

Instructions:

1. Preheat and Prepare:

- Preheat your oven to 350°F (175°C). Grease and flour a 9-inch round cake pan or line it with parchment paper.

2. Mix Dry Ingredients:

- In a bowl, sift together the buckwheat flour, all-purpose flour, baking powder, baking soda, and salt. If using ground cinnamon, add it to the dry ingredients.

3. Cream Butter and Sugar:

- In a separate large mixing bowl, cream together the softened butter and granulated sugar until light and fluffy.

4. Add Eggs and Honey:

- Beat in the eggs, one at a time, ensuring each is fully incorporated before adding the next. Then, mix in the honey until well combined.

5. Combine Wet and Dry Ingredients:

- Gradually add the dry ingredients to the butter mixture, alternating with buttermilk, beginning and ending with the flour mixture. Mix until just combined.

6. Bake the Cake:

- Pour the batter into the prepared cake pan, spreading it evenly with a spatula.
- Bake in the preheated oven for 30-35 minutes, or until a toothpick inserted into the center comes out clean.
- Remove from the oven and let the cake cool in the pan for 10 minutes before transferring it onto a wire rack to cool completely.

7. Decoration:

- Once the cake is completely cooled, dust the top with powdered sugar.

8. Serve:

- Slice and serve your Soba Cha Cake, enjoying the nutty flavor of buckwheat paired with honey and cinnamon.

This Soba Cha Cake recipe offers a unique and flavorful dessert option, perfect for those who appreciate the distinctive taste of buckwheat tea in a baked treat. Adjust the sweetness and spices according to your preference for a personalized culinary experience.

Japanese Pumpkin (Kabocha) Cake

Cake Base:

Kabocha Puree Cake:

- Use kabocha puree as the main ingredient to infuse the cake with its sweet and nutty flavor. Kabocha puree adds moisture and a rich texture to the cake.

Flavoring:

Warm Spices:

- Enhance the flavor profile with warm spices like cinnamon, nutmeg, and ginger, which complement the natural sweetness of kabocha.

Decoration:

Cream Cheese Frosting:

- Frost the cake with a tangy and creamy cream cheese frosting for a delightful contrast to the sweetness of the cake.

Optional Components:

Nuts or Seeds:

- Optionally, sprinkle chopped nuts or seeds on top of the cake for added texture and crunch.

Candied Kabocha:

- Garnish with candied kabocha slices or cubes for a decorative touch and extra sweetness.

Recipe: Japanese Pumpkin Cake

Ingredients:

For the Kabocha Cake:

- 1 cup kabocha squash puree (cooked and mashed)
- 1 1/2 cups all-purpose flour
- 1 teaspoon baking powder
- 1/2 teaspoon baking soda
- 1/2 teaspoon salt
- 1 teaspoon ground cinnamon
- 1/2 teaspoon ground nutmeg
- 1/2 teaspoon ground ginger
- 1/2 cup unsalted butter, softened
- 1 cup granulated sugar

- 2 large eggs
- 1 teaspoon vanilla extract
- 1/2 cup buttermilk (or 1/2 cup milk + 1/2 tablespoon lemon juice, let sit for 5 minutes)

For the Cream Cheese Frosting:

- 8 ounces cream cheese, softened
- 1/2 cup unsalted butter, softened
- 2 cups powdered sugar
- 1 teaspoon vanilla extract

Optional Garnish:

- Chopped nuts or seeds
- Candied kabocha slices or cubes

Instructions:

1. Prepare Kabocha Puree:

- Start by preparing the kabocha squash. Cut the kabocha in half, remove the seeds, and peel the skin. Cut into chunks and steam or boil until tender.
- Mash or puree the cooked kabocha until smooth. Measure out 1 cup of kabocha puree for the cake.

2. Preheat and Prepare:

- Preheat your oven to 350°F (175°C). Grease and flour a 9-inch round cake pan or line it with parchment paper.

3. Mix Dry Ingredients:

- In a bowl, sift together the flour, baking powder, baking soda, salt, cinnamon, nutmeg, and ginger. Set aside.

4. Cream Butter and Sugar:

- In a separate large mixing bowl, cream together the softened butter and granulated sugar until light and fluffy.

5. Add Eggs and Vanilla:

- Beat in the eggs, one at a time, ensuring each is fully incorporated before adding the next. Mix in the vanilla extract.

6. Combine Wet and Dry Ingredients:

- Gradually add the dry ingredients to the butter mixture, alternating with buttermilk, beginning and ending with the flour mixture. Mix until just combined.
- Fold in the kabocha puree until evenly incorporated into the batter.

7. Bake the Cake:

- Pour the batter into the prepared cake pan, spreading it evenly with a spatula.
- Bake in the preheated oven for 30-35 minutes, or until a toothpick inserted into the center comes out clean.
- Remove from the oven and let the cake cool in the pan for 10 minutes before transferring it onto a wire rack to cool completely.

8. Make the Cream Cheese Frosting:

- In a mixing bowl, beat the softened cream cheese and butter together until smooth and creamy.
- Gradually add the powdered sugar, mixing on low speed until incorporated. Beat in the vanilla extract until smooth and fluffy.

9. Frost and Decorate:

- Once the cake is completely cooled, frost the top and sides with the cream cheese frosting.
- Optionally, garnish with chopped nuts or seeds and candied kabocha slices or cubes for decoration.

10. Serve:

- Slice and serve your Japanese Pumpkin Cake, enjoying the unique flavor of kabocha squash combined with warm spices and creamy frosting.

This Japanese Pumpkin Cake recipe offers a delightful twist on traditional pumpkin desserts, highlighting the distinctive taste of kabocha squash in a moist and flavorful cake. Adjust the sweetness and spices according to your preference for a personalized culinary experience.

Amaou Strawberry Cake

Cake Base:

Sponge Cake Layers:

- Use light and airy sponge cake layers as the base to complement the freshness of Amaou strawberries.

Filling:

Fresh Amaou Strawberries and Whipped Cream:

- Layer fresh Amaou strawberries and whipped cream between the sponge cake layers. This combination highlights the natural sweetness and juiciness of the strawberries.

Decoration:

Additional Whipped Cream and Strawberries:

- Frost the cake with whipped cream and garnish with more fresh strawberries on top for a beautiful and delicious presentation.

Optional Components:

Strawberry Jam or Compote:

- Optionally, spread a thin layer of strawberry jam or compote between the cake layers for added sweetness and flavor.

Almond Slices or White Chocolate Shavings:

- Sprinkle toasted almond slices or white chocolate shavings on top of the cake for texture and visual appeal.

Recipe: Amaou Strawberry Cake

Ingredients:

For the Sponge Cake:

- 1 1/2 cups cake flour
- 1 teaspoon baking powder
- 1/4 teaspoon salt
- 4 large eggs
- 1 cup granulated sugar
- 1/2 cup whole milk
- 1/4 cup unsalted butter, melted and cooled
- 1 teaspoon vanilla extract

For the Filling and Decoration:

- 2 cups heavy cream, chilled
- 1/4 cup powdered sugar
- 1 teaspoon vanilla extract
- 2 cups fresh Amaou strawberries, hulled and sliced (plus extra for decoration)
- Optional: 1/2 cup strawberry jam or compote
- Optional: Toasted almond slices or white chocolate shavings, for garnish

Instructions:

1. Preheat and Prepare:

- Preheat your oven to 350°F (175°C). Grease and flour two 9-inch round cake pans or line them with parchment paper.

2. Make the Sponge Cake:

- In a bowl, sift together the cake flour, baking powder, and salt. Set aside.
- In another bowl, beat the eggs and granulated sugar with an electric mixer on high speed until pale and fluffy, about 5-7 minutes.
- Gently fold in the flour mixture in three additions, alternating with the milk, beginning and ending with the flour mixture.
- Fold in the melted butter and vanilla extract until just combined.
- Divide the batter evenly between the prepared cake pans and smooth the tops with a spatula.
- Bake in the preheated oven for 20-25 minutes, or until a toothpick inserted into the center of the cakes comes out clean.
- Remove from the oven and let the cakes cool in the pans for 10 minutes before transferring them to a wire rack to cool completely.

3. Prepare the Whipped Cream:

- In a chilled mixing bowl, whip the heavy cream, powdered sugar, and vanilla extract together until stiff peaks form.

4. Assemble the Cake:

- If using, spread a thin layer of strawberry jam or compote on one of the sponge cake layers.
- Spread a layer of whipped cream over the jam (if used) or directly on the cake layer.
- Arrange a layer of sliced Amaou strawberries over the whipped cream.
- Place the second sponge cake layer on top and gently press down.

5. Frost and Decorate:

- Frost the top and sides of the cake with the remaining whipped cream.
- Garnish the top with more fresh Amaou strawberries and sprinkle with toasted almond slices or white chocolate shavings if desired.

6. Chill and Serve:

- Refrigerate the cake for at least 1 hour before serving to allow the flavors to meld and the whipped cream to set.
- Slice and serve your Amaou Strawberry Cake, enjoying the fresh and fruity flavors with every bite.

This Amaou Strawberry Cake recipe captures the essence of these premium strawberries in a light and indulgent dessert. Adjust the sweetness and decorations according to your taste preferences for a delightful culinary experience.

Taiyaki-inspired Cake

Cake Base:

Vanilla Sponge Cake Layers:

- Use light and fluffy vanilla sponge cake layers as the base to mimic the soft texture of Taiyaki.

Filling:

Red Bean Paste and Custard Cream:

- Layer red bean paste and custard cream between the sponge cake layers to replicate the traditional fillings of Taiyaki. These fillings add sweetness and a creamy texture to the cake.

Decoration:

Fish-shaped Design:

- Shape the cake into a fish-like structure to resemble Taiyaki. You can achieve this by cutting the cake into a fish shape or using a fish-shaped cake mold.

Optional Components:

Chocolate Drizzle:

- Optionally, drizzle melted chocolate over the top of the cake for added richness and flavor.

Matcha Powder or Sesame Seeds:

- Sprinkle matcha powder or toasted sesame seeds on top of the cake for a decorative touch and added flavor.

Recipe: Taiyaki-inspired Cake

Ingredients:

For the Vanilla Sponge Cake:

- 2 cups cake flour
- 2 teaspoons baking powder
- 1/2 teaspoon salt
- 1 cup unsalted butter, softened
- 1 1/2 cups granulated sugar
- 4 large eggs
- 1 cup whole milk
- 1 teaspoon vanilla extract

For the Filling:

- 1 cup sweet red bean paste (anko)
- 1 cup custard cream (homemade or store-bought)

Optional Decoration:

- Melted chocolate, for drizzling
- Matcha powder or toasted sesame seeds, for sprinkling

Instructions:

1. Preheat and Prepare:

- Preheat your oven to 350°F (175°C). Grease and flour a 9x13-inch baking pan or line it with parchment paper.

2. Make the Vanilla Sponge Cake:

- In a bowl, sift together the cake flour, baking powder, and salt. Set aside.
- In another large mixing bowl, cream together the softened butter and granulated sugar until light and fluffy.
- Beat in the eggs, one at a time, ensuring each is fully incorporated before adding the next.
- Mix in the vanilla extract.
- Gradually add the flour mixture to the butter mixture, alternating with the milk, beginning and ending with the flour mixture. Mix until just combined.
- Pour the batter into the prepared baking pan, spreading it evenly with a spatula.
- Bake in the preheated oven for 25-30 minutes, or until a toothpick inserted into the center of the cake comes out clean.
- Remove from the oven and let the cake cool completely in the pan on a wire rack.

3. Assemble the Cake:

- Once cooled, remove the cake from the pan onto a cutting board.
- Using a fish-shaped cookie cutter or a sharp knife, cut out fish-shaped pieces from the cake. Alternatively, use a fish-shaped cake mold to bake the cake directly in the desired shape.
- Place one fish-shaped cake piece on a serving platter or cake stand.
- Spread a layer of sweet red bean paste (anko) over the cake piece.
- Top with a layer of custard cream.
- Place another fish-shaped cake piece on top and repeat the layers until all cake pieces are used, finishing with a final layer of custard cream on top.

4. Optional Decoration:

- If desired, drizzle melted chocolate over the top of the cake for added flavor and decoration.
- Sprinkle matcha powder or toasted sesame seeds on top of the cake for a decorative touch.

5. Chill and Serve:

- Refrigerate the Taiyaki-inspired Cake for at least 1 hour before serving to allow the flavors to meld and the fillings to set.

- Slice and serve your Taiyaki-inspired Cake, enjoying the flavors reminiscent of the beloved Japanese pastry in a delightful cake form.

This Taiyaki-inspired Cake recipe offers a fun and delicious twist on a classic Japanese treat, perfect for celebrations or themed parties. Customize the fillings and decorations according to your preferences for a unique culinary experience.

Shiroi Koibito-inspired Cake

Cake Base:

Vanilla Sponge Cake Layers:

- Use light and airy vanilla sponge cake layers as the base to mimic the soft and delicate texture of Shiroi Koibito.

Filling:

White Chocolate Mousse or Cream:

- Layer the cake with a luscious white chocolate mousse or cream filling. This filling captures the creamy sweetness of Shiroi Koibito's white chocolate.

Decoration:

White Chocolate Ganache or Glaze:

- Frost the cake with a smooth white chocolate ganache or glaze for a luxurious finish that mirrors the cookie's outer layer.

Optional Components:

Crushed Cookie Crust:

- Optionally, incorporate crushed Shiroi Koibito cookies into the cake layers for added texture and flavor.

Fresh Berries or Edible Flowers:

- Garnish the top of the cake with fresh berries or edible flowers for a decorative and flavorful touch.

Recipe: Shiroi Koibito-inspired Cake

Ingredients:

For the Vanilla Sponge Cake:

- 2 cups cake flour
- 2 teaspoons baking powder
- 1/2 teaspoon salt
- 1 cup unsalted butter, softened
- 1 1/2 cups granulated sugar
- 4 large eggs
- 1 cup whole milk
- 1 teaspoon vanilla extract

For the White Chocolate Mousse or Cream:

- 8 ounces white chocolate, chopped
- 1 1/2 cups heavy cream, chilled
- 1 teaspoon vanilla extract

For the White Chocolate Ganache or Glaze:

- 8 ounces white chocolate, chopped
- 1/2 cup heavy cream

Optional Garnish:

- Crushed Shiroi Koibito cookies
- Fresh berries or edible flowers

Instructions:

1. Preheat and Prepare:

- Preheat your oven to 350°F (175°C). Grease and flour two 9-inch round cake pans or line them with parchment paper.

2. Make the Vanilla Sponge Cake:

- In a bowl, sift together the cake flour, baking powder, and salt. Set aside.
- In another large mixing bowl, cream together the softened butter and granulated sugar until light and fluffy.
- Beat in the eggs, one at a time, ensuring each is fully incorporated before adding the next.
- Mix in the vanilla extract.
- Gradually add the flour mixture to the butter mixture, alternating with the milk, beginning and ending with the flour mixture. Mix until just combined.
- Divide the batter evenly between the prepared cake pans and smooth the tops with a spatula.
- Bake in the preheated oven for 25-30 minutes, or until a toothpick inserted into the center of the cakes comes out clean.
- Remove from the oven and let the cakes cool in the pans for 10 minutes before transferring them to a wire rack to cool completely.

3. Make the White Chocolate Mousse or Cream:

- In a heatproof bowl set over a saucepan of simmering water (double boiler method), melt the white chocolate, stirring until smooth. Remove from heat and let it cool to room temperature.
- In a chilled mixing bowl, whip the heavy cream and vanilla extract together until stiff peaks form.
- Gently fold the cooled melted white chocolate into the whipped cream until well combined. Refrigerate until ready to use.

4. Assemble the Cake:

- Place one cooled vanilla sponge cake layer on a serving platter or cake stand.
- Spread a layer of the white chocolate mousse or cream over the cake layer.

- Place the second vanilla sponge cake layer on top and gently press down.

5. Make the White Chocolate Ganache or Glaze:

- In a small saucepan, heat the heavy cream until it just begins to simmer.
- Remove from heat and add the chopped white chocolate. Let it sit for 1-2 minutes, then stir until smooth and creamy.
- Let the ganache or glaze cool slightly until it thickens but is still pourable.

6. Frost and Decorate:

- Pour the white chocolate ganache or glaze over the top of the cake, allowing it to drip down the sides.
- Optionally, sprinkle crushed Shiroi Koibito cookies over the top of the cake for added texture and flavor.

7. Optional Garnish:

- Garnish the top of the cake with fresh berries or edible flowers for a decorative touch.

8. Chill and Serve:

- Refrigerate the Shiroi Koibito-inspired Cake for at least 1 hour before serving to allow the flavors to meld and the fillings to set.
- Slice and serve your Shiroi Koibito-inspired Cake, savoring the luxurious combination of vanilla sponge, white chocolate mousse or cream, and white chocolate ganache.

This Shiroi Koibito-inspired Cake recipe offers a decadent twist on the beloved Hokkaido treat, perfect for special occasions or as a delightful dessert for white chocolate lovers. Adjust the decorations and garnishes according to your preferences for a personalized culinary experience.

Kyoto Uji Matcha Cake

Cake Base:

Matcha Sponge Cake Layers:

- Use light and fluffy matcha-infused sponge cake layers as the base to highlight the aromatic and slightly bitter notes of Uji matcha.

Filling:

Matcha Whipped Cream or White Chocolate Matcha Ganache:

- Layer the cake with matcha whipped cream or a smooth white chocolate matcha ganache. These fillings enhance the cake with a creamy texture and intense matcha flavor.

Decoration:

Matcha Cream Frosting:

- Frost the cake with a matcha-infused cream frosting for a vibrant green color and additional matcha flavor.

Optional Components:

Red Bean Paste (Anko) Filling:

- Optionally, spread a layer of sweet red bean paste (anko) between the cake layers for a traditional Japanese flavor combination.

Matcha Powder Dusting:

- Dust matcha powder over the top of the cake for a finishing touch and added matcha aroma.

Recipe: Kyoto Uji Matcha Cake

Ingredients:

For the Matcha Sponge Cake:

- 1 1/2 cups cake flour
- 2 teaspoons baking powder
- 1/2 teaspoon salt
- 1 tablespoon Uji matcha powder (high-quality matcha powder from Kyoto)
- 1/2 cup unsalted butter, softened
- 1 cup granulated sugar
- 3 large eggs
- 1 teaspoon vanilla extract
- 1/2 cup whole milk

For the Matcha Whipped Cream:

- 2 cups heavy cream, chilled
- 1/4 cup powdered sugar
- 1 tablespoon Uji matcha powder

For the Matcha Cream Frosting:

- 8 ounces cream cheese, softened
- 1/2 cup unsalted butter, softened
- 2 cups powdered sugar
- 1 tablespoon Uji matcha powder

Optional Filling:

- 1 cup sweet red bean paste (anko)

Optional Garnish:

- Uji matcha powder, for dusting

Instructions:

1. Preheat and Prepare:

- Preheat your oven to 350°F (175°C). Grease and flour two 9-inch round cake pans or line them with parchment paper.

2. Make the Matcha Sponge Cake:

- In a bowl, sift together the cake flour, baking powder, salt, and Uji matcha powder. Set aside.
- In another large mixing bowl, cream together the softened butter and granulated sugar until light and fluffy.
- Beat in the eggs, one at a time, ensuring each is fully incorporated before adding the next.
- Mix in the vanilla extract.
- Gradually add the flour mixture to the butter mixture, alternating with the milk, beginning and ending with the flour mixture. Mix until just combined.
- Divide the batter evenly between the prepared cake pans and smooth the tops with a spatula.
- Bake in the preheated oven for 25-30 minutes, or until a toothpick inserted into the center of the cakes comes out clean.
- Remove from the oven and let the cakes cool in the pans for 10 minutes before transferring them to a wire rack to cool completely.

3. Make the Matcha Whipped Cream:

- In a chilled mixing bowl, whip the heavy cream, powdered sugar, and Uji matcha powder together until stiff peaks form.

4. Make the Matcha Cream Frosting:

- In another mixing bowl, beat the softened cream cheese and butter together until smooth and creamy.
- Gradually add the powdered sugar and Uji matcha powder, mixing on low speed until incorporated. Increase speed and beat until smooth and fluffy.

5. Assemble the Cake:

- If using, spread a layer of sweet red bean paste (anko) on one of the matcha sponge cake layers.
- Spread a layer of matcha whipped cream over the anko layer or directly on the cake layer.
- Place the second matcha sponge cake layer on top and gently press down.

6. Frost the Cake:

- Frost the top and sides of the cake with the matcha cream frosting, smoothing it evenly with a spatula.

7. Optional Garnish:

- Dust the top of the cake with Uji matcha powder for a decorative finish.

8. Chill and Serve:

- Refrigerate the Kyoto Uji Matcha Cake for at least 1 hour before serving to allow the flavors to meld and the frosting to set.
- Slice and serve your Kyoto Uji Matcha Cake, savoring the authentic flavors of Uji matcha in a delightful and creamy dessert.

This Kyoto Uji Matcha Cake recipe brings together the elegance of Uji matcha with the indulgence of a layered cake, perfect for special occasions or as a treat for matcha enthusiasts. Adjust the sweetness and decorations according to your preferences for a personalized culinary experience.

Japanese Honey Castella

Ingredients:

- 6 large eggs, at room temperature
- 150 grams (3/4 cup) granulated sugar
- 100 grams (1/3 cup) honey
- 100 ml (1/3 cup + 1 tablespoon) whole milk, warmed
- 100 grams (3/4 cup) cake flour
- 25 grams (2 tablespoons) cornstarch
- 1/4 teaspoon salt
- 1 teaspoon vanilla extract

Instructions:

1. Preheat and Prepare:

- Preheat your oven to 325°F (160°C). Grease and line a 9x5 inch (23x13 cm) loaf pan with parchment paper.

2. Warm the Milk:

- In a small saucepan, warm the milk until it's just heated but not boiling. Remove from heat and set aside.

3. Separate and Beat Eggs:

- Separate the egg yolks from the whites. In a large mixing bowl, beat the egg yolks with sugar and honey until pale and thickened.

4. Add Milk and Vanilla:

- Gradually add the warmed milk and vanilla extract to the egg yolk mixture, mixing until well combined.

5. Sift Dry Ingredients:

- Sift together the cake flour, cornstarch, and salt. Gradually add this dry mixture to the egg yolk mixture, stirring until smooth. Set aside.

6. Whip Egg Whites:

- In another clean bowl, whip the egg whites with a hand mixer or stand mixer until soft peaks form.

7. Fold Batter Together:

- Gently fold the whipped egg whites into the egg yolk batter in three additions, folding until just combined. Be gentle to maintain the airiness of the batter.

8. Bake the Cake:

- Pour the batter into the prepared loaf pan, gently tapping the pan on the counter to release any air bubbles.
- Bake in the preheated oven for 50-60 minutes, or until a toothpick inserted into the center of the cake comes out clean.

9. Cool and Serve:

- Remove the cake from the oven and let it cool in the pan for 10 minutes. Then, transfer the cake to a wire rack to cool completely.

10. Slice and Enjoy:

- Once cooled, slice the Japanese Honey Castella cake into pieces and serve. It can be enjoyed plain or with a dusting of powdered sugar on top.

Tips for Making Japanese Honey Castella Cake:

- **Egg Temperature:** Make sure your eggs are at room temperature for easier whipping and better volume.
- **Folding Technique:** When folding the whipped egg whites into the batter, use a gentle folding motion to avoid deflating the mixture.
- **Baking Time:** Oven temperatures may vary, so keep an eye on the cake after 50 minutes. It should be golden brown on top and a toothpick inserted into the center should come out clean when done.

Japanese Honey Castella cake is known for its soft texture and subtle sweetness, making it a delightful treat for any occasion. Enjoy baking and savoring this traditional Japanese dessert!

Warabi Mochi Cake

Ingredients:

- 100 grams (3.5 oz) warabi mochi powder (bracken starch)
- 200 grams (7 oz) granulated sugar
- 600 ml (2.5 cups) water
- 1 tablespoon kinako (roasted soybean flour), for dusting
- Optional: kuromitsu (brown sugar syrup) and additional kinako for serving

Instructions:

1. Prepare the Warabi Mochi Batter:

- In a large mixing bowl, combine the warabi mochi powder and granulated sugar.
- Gradually add the water to the dry ingredients, stirring continuously to prevent lumps.

2. Cook the Mixture:

- Pour the mixture into a saucepan and cook over medium heat, stirring constantly with a whisk or wooden spoon.
- Continue stirring until the mixture thickens and becomes translucent, similar to a pudding consistency. This usually takes about 10-15 minutes.

3. Transfer to a Mold:

- Once the mixture is thickened, quickly pour it into a rectangular or square mold lined with plastic wrap or parchment paper. Smooth out the top with a spatula.

4. Chill and Set:

- Let the warabi mochi mixture cool to room temperature. Then, refrigerate it for at least 1-2 hours, or until completely set and firm.

5. Serve:

- Once chilled and set, remove the warabi mochi cake from the mold and cut it into squares or rectangles.
- Dust the pieces with kinako (roasted soybean flour) before serving.
- Optionally, drizzle with kuromitsu (brown sugar syrup) and sprinkle with more kinako for added flavor.

Tips for Making Warabi Mochi Cake:

- **Warabi Mochi Powder:** Ensure you use authentic warabi mochi powder (bracken starch), which is essential for the unique texture and consistency of the cake.
- **Consistency:** Stir the mixture constantly while cooking to prevent clumps and ensure a smooth, even texture.

- **Chilling:** Refrigerate the cake until it's well set before cutting into pieces. This allows the mochi to firm up and hold its shape.
- **Storage:** Store any leftover Warabi Mochi Cake pieces in an airtight container in the refrigerator. It's best enjoyed within a few days for optimal freshness.

Warabi Mochi Cake offers a delightful chewy texture and a subtly sweet flavor, making it a popular treat in Japanese cuisine. Enjoy this unique dessert as a refreshing and satisfying snack or dessert option!

Daifuku Mochi Cake

Ingredients:

For the Cake Layers:

- 1 1/2 cups glutinous rice flour (mochiko)
- 1/2 cup granulated sugar
- 1 teaspoon baking powder
- 1/4 teaspoon salt
- 3/4 cup whole milk
- 1/4 cup vegetable oil
- 1 teaspoon vanilla extract

For the Filling:

- 1 cup sweet red bean paste (anko)

Optional Garnish:

- Powdered sugar, for dusting

Instructions:

1. Preheat and Prepare:

- Preheat your oven to 350°F (175°C). Grease and line an 8-inch round cake pan with parchment paper.

2. Make the Cake Layers:

- In a large mixing bowl, whisk together the glutinous rice flour (mochiko), granulated sugar, baking powder, and salt.
- In a separate bowl, whisk together the whole milk, vegetable oil, and vanilla extract.
- Gradually add the wet ingredients to the dry ingredients, stirring until smooth and well combined.
- Pour the batter into the prepared cake pan, spreading it evenly with a spatula.
- Bake in the preheated oven for 25-30 minutes, or until a toothpick inserted into the center of the cake comes out clean.
- Remove from the oven and let the cake cool in the pan for 10 minutes. Then, transfer it to a wire rack to cool completely.

3. Assemble the Daifuku Mochi Cake:

- Once the cake is completely cooled, carefully slice it horizontally into two even layers.
- Place one cake layer on a serving platter or cake stand.
- Spread a generous layer of sweet red bean paste (anko) over the top of the cake layer.
- Place the second cake layer on top of the filling, gently pressing down to secure.

4. Optional Garnish:

- Dust the top of the Daifuku Mochi Cake with powdered sugar for a decorative finish.

5. Serve and Enjoy:

- Slice and serve the Daifuku Mochi Cake, savoring the combination of soft mochi cake layers and sweet red bean paste filling.

Tips for Making Daifuku Mochi Cake:

- **Glutinous Rice Flour (Mochiko):** Use mochiko specifically for this recipe to achieve the characteristic chewy texture of mochi.
- **Filling Variations:** Experiment with different fillings such as matcha cream, strawberries, or other fruit preserves for a unique twist.
- **Storage:** Store any leftovers in an airtight container in the refrigerator. Enjoy within a few days for the best taste and texture.

Daifuku Mochi Cake offers a delightful fusion of traditional Japanese flavors in a cake form, perfect for celebrations or as a special treat. Enjoy this unique dessert with friends and family!

Kuri Kinton (Chestnut Sweet) Cake

Ingredients:

For the Cake Layers:

- 1 1/2 cups cake flour
- 1 1/2 teaspoons baking powder
- 1/4 teaspoon salt
- 1/2 cup unsalted butter, softened
- 1 cup granulated sugar
- 3 large eggs
- 1 teaspoon vanilla extract
- 1/2 cup whole milk

For the Kuri Kinton Filling:

- 500 grams (about 1 lb) fresh chestnuts or canned chestnuts
- 1 cup granulated sugar
- 1/2 cup water
- Pinch of salt

Optional Garnish:

- Whipped cream
- Crushed or chopped chestnuts (for topping)

Instructions:

1. Prepare the Chestnuts:

- If using fresh chestnuts, score an "X" on the flat side of each chestnut with a knife. Boil them for about 15-20 minutes until tender. Peel off the shells and inner skin while they're still warm. If using canned chestnuts, skip this step.

2. Make the Kuri Kinton Filling:

- In a saucepan, combine the boiled (or canned) chestnuts, sugar, water, and a pinch of salt.
- Cook over medium heat, stirring occasionally, until the chestnuts are soft and the liquid has reduced to a thick syrupy consistency, about 15-20 minutes.
- Mash the chestnuts with a fork or potato masher until smooth and spreadable. Remove from heat and let it cool completely.

3. Preheat and Prepare:

- Preheat your oven to 350°F (175°C). Grease and flour two 9-inch round cake pans or line them with parchment paper.

4. Make the Cake Layers:

- In a bowl, sift together the cake flour, baking powder, and salt. Set aside.
- In another large mixing bowl, cream together the softened butter and granulated sugar until light and fluffy.
- Beat in the eggs, one at a time, ensuring each is fully incorporated before adding the next. Mix in the vanilla extract.
- Gradually add the flour mixture to the butter mixture, alternating with the milk, beginning and ending with the flour mixture. Mix until just combined.
- Divide the batter evenly between the prepared cake pans and smooth the tops with a spatula.
- Bake in the preheated oven for 25-30 minutes, or until a toothpick inserted into the center of the cakes comes out clean.
- Remove from the oven and let the cakes cool in the pans for 10 minutes before transferring them to a wire rack to cool completely.

5. Assemble the Kuri Kinton Cake:

- Once the cake layers are completely cooled, place one layer on a serving platter or cake stand.
- Spread a generous layer of the cooled Kuri Kinton filling over the top of the cake layer.
- Place the second cake layer on top and gently press down.

6. Optional Garnish:

- Garnish the top of the cake with whipped cream and sprinkle crushed or chopped chestnuts over the top for added texture and flavor.

7. Serve and Enjoy:

- Slice and serve your Kuri Kinton Cake, savoring the sweet chestnut filling and soft cake layers.

Tips for Making Kuri Kinton Cake:

- **Chestnut Preparation:** Ensure the chestnuts are cooked until soft and mashed thoroughly to achieve a smooth filling consistency.
- **Cake Texture:** The cake should be light and fluffy, complementing the rich and sweet Kuri Kinton filling.
- **Storage:** Store any leftover Kuri Kinton Cake in an airtight container in the refrigerator. Enjoy within a few days for the best taste and texture.

Kuri Kinton Cake offers a delightful fusion of cake and traditional Japanese sweet flavors, making it a perfect dessert for special occasions or as a treat for chestnut lovers. Enjoy this unique dessert with family and friends!

Kasutera (Japanese Honey Sponge Cake)

Ingredients:

- 4 large eggs, at room temperature
- 150 grams (3/4 cup) granulated sugar
- 60 grams (1/4 cup) honey
- 1 teaspoon vanilla extract
- 80 ml (1/3 cup) whole milk
- 1 tablespoon vegetable oil
- 120 grams (1 cup) cake flour
- 1/2 teaspoon baking powder

Instructions:

1. Preheat and Prepare:

- Preheat your oven to 320°F (160°C). Grease and line a 9x5 inch (23x13 cm) loaf pan with parchment paper.

2. Prepare the Batter:

- In a small saucepan, warm the milk and honey over low heat until the honey is melted. Remove from heat and set aside to cool slightly.
- In a large mixing bowl, beat the eggs and granulated sugar together with a hand mixer or stand mixer until pale and fluffy.
- Add the vanilla extract and beat until combined.
- Gradually add the milk and honey mixture, followed by the vegetable oil, mixing on low speed until incorporated.
- Sift the cake flour and baking powder into the batter. Gently fold in with a spatula until just combined. Do not overmix.

3. Bake the Cake:

- Pour the batter into the prepared loaf pan, smoothing the top with a spatula.
- Tap the pan gently on the counter to release any air bubbles.
- Bake in the preheated oven for 50-60 minutes, or until a toothpick inserted into the center of the cake comes out clean.

4. Cool and Serve:

- Remove the cake from the oven and let it cool in the pan for 10 minutes.
- Transfer the cake to a wire rack to cool completely before slicing.

5. Optional: Dusting with Powdered Sugar

- Once cooled, dust the top of the Kasutera with powdered sugar for a decorative finish.

6. Slice and Enjoy:

- Slice the Kasutera into pieces and serve. It can be enjoyed plain or with a cup of tea or coffee.

Tips for Making Kasutera:

- **Egg Temperature:** Ensure your eggs are at room temperature for better incorporation and volume.
- **Mixing Technique:** When folding in the flour, use gentle, folding motions to avoid deflating the batter.
- **Storage:** Store any leftover Kasutera in an airtight container at room temperature for up to 3 days. It can also be frozen for longer storage.

Kasutera is a classic Japanese dessert known for its delicate texture and subtle sweetness. Enjoy making and savoring this delightful Japanese honey sponge cake at home!

Okinawan Sweet Potato Cake

Ingredients:

- 2 cups mashed Okinawan sweet potatoes (about 2 medium-sized potatoes)
- 3/4 cup granulated sugar
- 1/2 cup unsalted butter, melted
- 3 large eggs
- 1/2 cup whole milk
- 1 teaspoon vanilla extract
- 1 1/2 cups all-purpose flour
- 2 teaspoons baking powder
- 1/4 teaspoon salt
- Optional: powdered sugar for dusting

Instructions:

1. Prepare the Okinawan Sweet Potatoes:

- Wash and peel the sweet potatoes. Cut them into chunks and steam or boil until tender.
- Mash the cooked sweet potatoes until smooth. Measure out 2 cups of mashed sweet potatoes for the recipe.

2. Preheat and Prepare:

- Preheat your oven to 350°F (175°C). Grease and flour a 9-inch round cake pan or line it with parchment paper for easy removal.

3. Make the Cake Batter:

- In a large mixing bowl, combine the mashed sweet potatoes, granulated sugar, melted butter, eggs, milk, and vanilla extract. Mix until well combined and smooth.
- In a separate bowl, sift together the all-purpose flour, baking powder, and salt.
- Gradually add the dry ingredients to the sweet potato mixture, mixing until just combined. Be careful not to overmix.

4. Bake the Cake:

- Pour the batter into the prepared cake pan, smoothing the top with a spatula.
- Bake in the preheated oven for 30-35 minutes, or until a toothpick inserted into the center of the cake comes out clean.

5. Cool and Serve:

- Remove the cake from the oven and let it cool in the pan for 10 minutes.
- Transfer the cake to a wire rack to cool completely.

6. Optional: Dusting with Powdered Sugar

- Once cooled, dust the top of the Okinawan Sweet Potato Cake with powdered sugar for a decorative touch.

7. Slice and Enjoy:

- Slice the cake into pieces and serve. This cake pairs well with a hot cup of tea or coffee.

Tips for Making Okinawan Sweet Potato Cake:

- **Sweet Potatoes:** Use Okinawan sweet potatoes for their distinct purple color and sweet flavor. If unavailable, regular sweet potatoes can be substituted.
- **Texture:** The cake should have a moist and tender texture due to the mashed sweet potatoes. Ensure they are well mashed to avoid lumps.
- **Storage:** Store any leftover cake in an airtight container at room temperature for up to 3 days. It can also be refrigerated for longer freshness.

Okinawan Sweet Potato Cake offers a unique twist on traditional cakes with its vibrant color and delightful sweetness. Enjoy making and sharing this special dessert with family and friends!

Ichigo Roll Cake

Sponge Cake Ingredients:

- 4 large eggs, at room temperature
- 100 grams (1/2 cup) granulated sugar
- 100 grams (3/4 cup) cake flour
- 1 tablespoon milk
- 1 teaspoon vanilla extract
- Pinch of salt

Filling Ingredients:

- 200 ml (about 1 cup) heavy cream
- 2 tablespoons granulated sugar
- Fresh strawberries, sliced

Optional Garnish:

- Powdered sugar, for dusting
- Additional fresh strawberries, for decoration

Instructions:

1. Preheat and Prepare:

- Preheat your oven to 350°F (175°C). Line a 10x15 inch (25x38 cm) jelly roll pan with parchment paper, leaving some overhang on the sides.

2. Prepare the Sponge Cake:

- In a large mixing bowl, beat the eggs and granulated sugar with a hand mixer or stand mixer until pale, fluffy, and tripled in volume. This usually takes about 5-7 minutes.
- Sift the cake flour into the egg mixture in two additions, gently folding it in with a spatula after each addition until just combined.
- Mix in the milk, vanilla extract, and pinch of salt, folding gently until the batter is smooth and well combined.

3. Bake the Sponge Cake:

- Pour the batter into the prepared jelly roll pan, spreading it evenly with a spatula to the edges.
- Bake in the preheated oven for 12-15 minutes, or until the top is lightly golden and springs back when gently pressed.

4. Roll the Cake:

- While the cake is baking, lay out a clean kitchen towel and dust it lightly with powdered sugar.
- Once the cake is done, immediately invert it onto the prepared towel. Carefully peel off the parchment paper.

- Starting from one short end, gently roll the cake and towel together into a tight spiral. Place seam-side down on a wire rack and let it cool completely.

5. Prepare the Filling:

- In a chilled mixing bowl, whip the heavy cream and granulated sugar until stiff peaks form.

6. Assemble the Roll Cake:

- Carefully unroll the cooled cake from the towel. Spread the whipped cream evenly over the surface of the cake.
- Arrange the sliced fresh strawberries evenly over the whipped cream.
- Gently roll the cake back up, this time without the towel. Place seam-side down on a serving platter.

7. Optional Garnish:

- Dust the top of the Ichigo Roll Cake with powdered sugar.
- Garnish with additional fresh strawberries for decoration if desired.

8. Chill and Serve:

- Refrigerate the roll cake for at least 1 hour before serving to set the filling and make slicing easier.

9. Slice and Enjoy:

- Slice the Ichigo Roll Cake into pieces using a sharp knife. Serve chilled and enjoy!

Tips for Making Ichigo Roll Cake:

- **Egg Temperature:** It's essential to use eggs at room temperature for better volume and texture when beating with sugar.
- **Rolling Technique:** Roll the cake while it's still warm to prevent cracking. Use a kitchen towel dusted with powdered sugar to help with rolling.
- **Filling Variations:** Experiment with different fillings such as custard, chocolate ganache, or other fruits like raspberries or blueberries for variety.

Ichigo Roll Cake is a delightful dessert, perfect for celebrations or as a sweet treat. Enjoy making and savoring this Japanese-style strawberry roll cake with friends and family!

Dorayaki Roll Cake

Sponge Cake Ingredients:

- 4 large eggs, at room temperature
- 100 grams (1/2 cup) granulated sugar
- 100 grams (3/4 cup) cake flour
- 1 tablespoon milk
- 1 teaspoon vanilla extract
- Pinch of salt

Filling Ingredients:

- 200 ml (about 1 cup) heavy cream
- 2 tablespoons granulated sugar
- Red bean paste (anko) or Nutella (as per preference)

Optional Garnish:

- Powdered sugar, for dusting
- Additional toppings like sliced strawberries or matcha powder (optional)

Instructions:

1. Preheat and Prepare:

- Preheat your oven to 350°F (175°C). Line a 10x15 inch (25x38 cm) jelly roll pan with parchment paper, leaving some overhang on the sides.

2. Prepare the Sponge Cake:

- In a large mixing bowl, beat the eggs and granulated sugar with a hand mixer or stand mixer until pale, fluffy, and tripled in volume. This usually takes about 5-7 minutes.
- Sift the cake flour into the egg mixture in two additions, gently folding it in with a spatula after each addition until just combined.
- Mix in the milk, vanilla extract, and pinch of salt, folding gently until the batter is smooth and well combined.

3. Bake the Sponge Cake:

- Pour the batter into the prepared jelly roll pan, spreading it evenly with a spatula to the edges.
- Bake in the preheated oven for 12-15 minutes, or until the top is lightly golden and springs back when gently pressed.

4. Roll the Cake:

- While the cake is baking, lay out a clean kitchen towel and dust it lightly with powdered sugar.
- Once the cake is done, immediately invert it onto the prepared towel. Carefully peel off the parchment paper.

- Starting from one short end, gently roll the cake and towel together into a tight spiral. Place seam-side down on a wire rack and let it cool completely.

5. Prepare the Filling:

- In a chilled mixing bowl, whip the heavy cream and granulated sugar until stiff peaks form.

6. Assemble the Roll Cake:

- Carefully unroll the cooled cake from the towel. Spread the red bean paste (anko) or Nutella evenly over the surface of the cake.
- Spread the whipped cream evenly over the red bean paste (anko) or Nutella.
- Gently roll the cake back up, this time without the towel. Place seam-side down on a serving platter.

7. Optional Garnish:

- Dust the top of the Dorayaki Roll Cake with powdered sugar.
- Optionally, garnish with additional toppings like sliced strawberries or a sprinkle of matcha powder for decoration.

8. Chill and Serve:

- Refrigerate the roll cake for at least 1 hour before serving to set the filling and make slicing easier.

9. Slice and Enjoy:

- Slice the Dorayaki Roll Cake into pieces using a sharp knife. Serve chilled and enjoy the delightful combination of fluffy sponge cake, creamy filling, and sweet red bean paste (anko) or Nutella!

Tips for Making Dorayaki Roll Cake:

- **Egg Temperature:** It's essential to use eggs at room temperature for better volume and texture when beating with sugar.
- **Rolling Technique:** Roll the cake while it's still warm to prevent cracking. Use a kitchen towel dusted with powdered sugar to help with rolling.
- **Filling Variations:** Customize the filling with your favorite spread—traditional red bean paste (anko) for a classic Dorayaki flavor or Nutella for a chocolate twist.

Dorayaki Roll Cake offers a delightful fusion of traditional Japanese flavors and cake-making techniques. Enjoy making and savoring this unique dessert with family and friends!

Karinto (Japanese Fried Dough) Cake

Cake Ingredients:

- 1 1/2 cups all-purpose flour
- 1 teaspoon baking powder
- 1/2 teaspoon baking soda
- 1/4 teaspoon salt
- 1/2 cup unsalted butter, softened
- 3/4 cup brown sugar
- 2 large eggs
- 1 teaspoon vanilla extract
- 1/2 cup sour cream
- 1/4 cup milk

Karinto Topping Ingredients:

- 1/2 cup brown sugar
- 1/4 cup soy sauce
- 1/4 cup water
- 1/4 teaspoon baking soda
- Vegetable oil, for frying
- Powdered sugar, for dusting (optional)

Instructions:

1. Prepare the Karinto Topping:

- In a small saucepan, combine the brown sugar, soy sauce, water, and baking soda.
- Heat over medium-high heat, stirring constantly, until the mixture reaches a boil. Reduce the heat and simmer for about 3-4 minutes until slightly thickened.
- Remove from heat and let it cool to room temperature. The mixture will thicken as it cools.

2. Prepare the Cake:

- Preheat your oven to 350°F (175°C). Grease and flour a 9-inch round cake pan or line it with parchment paper.
- In a medium bowl, whisk together the flour, baking powder, baking soda, and salt. Set aside.
- In a large mixing bowl, cream together the softened butter and brown sugar until light and fluffy.
- Add the eggs one at a time, beating well after each addition. Mix in the vanilla extract.
- Gradually add the dry ingredients to the butter mixture, alternating with the sour cream and milk. Begin and end with the dry ingredients, mixing until just combined.

3. Bake the Cake:

- Pour the batter into the prepared cake pan, spreading it evenly with a spatula.
- Bake in the preheated oven for 25-30 minutes, or until a toothpick inserted into the center of the cake comes out clean.

- Remove from the oven and let the cake cool in the pan for 10 minutes. Then transfer it to a wire rack to cool completely.

4. Fry the Karinto Topping:

- In a medium skillet or frying pan, heat vegetable oil over medium-high heat until it reaches 350°F (175°C).
- Drop small spoonfuls of the Karinto topping mixture into the hot oil, frying in batches for about 1-2 minutes per side or until golden brown and crispy.
- Remove the fried Karinto pieces with a slotted spoon and place them on a paper towel-lined plate to drain excess oil.

5. Assemble the Karinto Cake:

- Once the cake has cooled completely, spread the fried Karinto pieces evenly over the top of the cake.
- Optionally, dust the cake with powdered sugar for a decorative finish.

6. Slice and Serve:

- Slice the Karinto Cake into pieces and serve. Enjoy the unique blend of flavors from the brown sugar, soy sauce, and crispy fried dough topping!

Tips for Making Karinto Cake:

- **Oil Temperature:** Maintain a consistent frying temperature to achieve crispy Karinto pieces without burning.
- **Frying Safety:** Be cautious when frying the Karinto topping as hot oil can splatter. Use a slotted spoon for safe removal from the oil.
- **Storage:** Store any leftover Karinto Cake in an airtight container. The fried Karinto topping may soften over time, so enjoy it fresh for the best texture.

Karinto Cake combines the sweetness of cake with the savory crunch of traditional Japanese fried dough, making it a delightful and unique dessert option. Enjoy making and sharing this flavorful treat with family and friends!

Zunda (Sweetened Edamame Paste) Cake

Cake Ingredients:

- 1 cup all-purpose flour
- 1 teaspoon baking powder
- 1/4 teaspoon baking soda
- 1/4 teaspoon salt
- 1/2 cup unsalted butter, softened
- 3/4 cup granulated sugar
- 2 large eggs
- 1 teaspoon vanilla extract
- 1/2 cup plain Greek yogurt
- 1/4 cup milk

Zunda Filling Ingredients:

- 1 cup shelled edamame (frozen or fresh)
- 1/4 cup granulated sugar (adjust to taste)
- 2-3 tablespoons milk (adjust consistency)
- 1 tablespoon unsalted butter, softened

Optional Garnish:

- Powdered sugar, for dusting
- Sliced almonds or pistachios, for decoration

Instructions:

1. Prepare the Zunda Filling:

- Cook the shelled edamame according to package instructions until tender. Drain and rinse under cold water to cool.
- In a food processor or blender, combine the cooked edamame, granulated sugar, milk, and softened butter. Blend until smooth and creamy, adding more milk as needed to achieve a spreadable consistency. Taste and adjust sweetness if desired.

2. Prepare the Cake:

- Preheat your oven to 350°F (175°C). Grease and flour a 9-inch round cake pan or line it with parchment paper.
- In a medium bowl, whisk together the flour, baking powder, baking soda, and salt. Set aside.
- In a large mixing bowl, cream together the softened butter and granulated sugar until light and fluffy.
- Add the eggs one at a time, beating well after each addition. Mix in the vanilla extract.
- Gradually add the dry ingredients to the butter mixture, alternating with the Greek yogurt and milk. Begin and end with the dry ingredients, mixing until just combined.

3. Assemble the Zunda Cake:

- Pour half of the cake batter into the prepared cake pan, spreading it evenly with a spatula.
- Spoon the Zunda filling over the batter, spreading it evenly to cover.
- Carefully spoon the remaining cake batter over the Zunda filling, spreading it gently to cover the filling completely.

4. Bake the Cake:

- Bake in the preheated oven for 30-35 minutes, or until a toothpick inserted into the center of the cake comes out clean.
- Remove from the oven and let the cake cool in the pan for 10 minutes. Then transfer it to a wire rack to cool completely.

5. Optional Garnish:

- Dust the top of the Zunda Cake with powdered sugar.
- Garnish with sliced almonds or pistachios for a decorative touch.

6. Slice and Serve:

- Slice the Zunda Cake into pieces and serve. Enjoy the unique and delicious flavor of sweetened edamame paste combined with moist cake!

Tips for Making Zunda Cake:

- **Edamame Paste Consistency:** Adjust the milk amount in the Zunda filling to achieve a spreadable consistency. It should be smooth and creamy but not too runny.
- **Cake Texture:** Be careful not to overmix the cake batter once the dry ingredients are added to ensure a tender texture.
- **Storage:** Store any leftover Zunda Cake in an airtight container in the refrigerator for up to 3 days. Bring to room temperature before serving for best flavor.

Zunda Cake offers a delightful twist on traditional cakes with its unique use of sweetened edamame paste. Enjoy making and sharing this flavorful Japanese-inspired dessert with family and friends!

Sata Andagi (Okinawan Donut) CakeHimono Cake

Cake Ingredients:

- 2 cups all-purpose flour
- 2 teaspoons baking powder
- 1/2 teaspoon baking soda
- 1/4 teaspoon salt
- 1 cup granulated sugar
- 1/2 cup unsalted butter, softened
- 3 large eggs
- 1 cup plain Greek yogurt
- 1/4 cup milk
- 1 teaspoon vanilla extract

Sata Andagi Glaze Ingredients:

- 1 cup powdered sugar
- 2-3 tablespoons milk
- 1/2 teaspoon vanilla extract

Optional Garnish:

- Powdered sugar, for dusting
- Chopped nuts (such as walnuts or almonds), for decoration

Instructions:

1. Prepare the Cake:

- Preheat your oven to 350°F (175°C). Grease and flour a 9-inch round cake pan or line it with parchment paper.
- In a medium bowl, whisk together the flour, baking powder, baking soda, and salt. Set aside.
- In a large mixing bowl, cream together the softened butter and granulated sugar until light and fluffy.
- Add the eggs one at a time, beating well after each addition. Mix in the vanilla extract.
- Gradually add the dry ingredients to the butter mixture, alternating with the Greek yogurt and milk. Begin and end with the dry ingredients, mixing until just combined.

2. Bake the Cake:

- Pour the batter into the prepared cake pan, spreading it evenly with a spatula.
- Bake in the preheated oven for 30-35 minutes, or until a toothpick inserted into the center of the cake comes out clean.
- Remove from the oven and let the cake cool in the pan for 10 minutes. Then transfer it to a wire rack to cool completely.

3. Prepare the Sata Andagi Glaze:

- In a small bowl, whisk together the powdered sugar, milk, and vanilla extract until smooth and glossy. Adjust the consistency by adding more milk if needed.

4. Glaze the Cake:

- Once the cake has cooled completely, drizzle the Sata Andagi glaze over the top of the cake, allowing it to drip down the sides.

5. Optional Garnish:

- Dust the top of the Sata Andagi Cake with powdered sugar.
- Sprinkle chopped nuts over the glaze for added texture and decoration.

6. Slice and Serve:

- Slice the Sata Andagi Cake into pieces and serve. Enjoy the delightful combination of flavors and textures reminiscent of traditional Okinawan Sata Andagi!

Tips for Making Sata Andagi Cake:

- **Greek Yogurt:** Greek yogurt adds moisture and a slight tanginess to the cake. You can substitute with sour cream if preferred.
- **Glaze Consistency:** Adjust the milk amount in the glaze to achieve your desired consistency. It should be thin enough to drizzle but thick enough to coat the cake.
- **Storage:** Store any leftover Sata Andagi Cake in an airtight container at room temperature for up to 3 days. Refresh the glaze before serving if needed.

Sata Andagi Cake offers a delicious twist on traditional Okinawan sweets, combining the flavors of a beloved fried treat with the ease of a cake. Enjoy making and sharing this unique dessert with family and friends!

Himono Cake

Cake Ingredients:

- 2 cups all-purpose flour
- 2 teaspoons baking powder
- 1/2 teaspoon baking soda
- 1/2 teaspoon salt
- 1/2 cup unsalted butter, softened
- 1 cup granulated sugar
- 3 large eggs
- 1 cup plain Greek yogurt
- 1/4 cup milk
- 1 teaspoon vanilla extract
- 1/2 cup chopped dried fish (himono), such as mackerel or sardines, finely chopped

Optional Savory Glaze Ingredients:

- 1/2 cup powdered sugar
- 2-3 tablespoons soy sauce or tamari
- 1 tablespoon mirin (Japanese sweet rice wine)
- 1 tablespoon water

Optional Garnish:

- Chopped green onions or chives, for decoration

Instructions:

1. Prepare the Cake:

- Preheat your oven to 350°F (175°C). Grease and flour a 9-inch round cake pan or line it with parchment paper.
- In a medium bowl, whisk together the flour, baking powder, baking soda, and salt. Set aside.
- In a large mixing bowl, cream together the softened butter and granulated sugar until light and fluffy.
- Add the eggs one at a time, beating well after each addition. Mix in the vanilla extract.
- Gradually add the dry ingredients to the butter mixture, alternating with the Greek yogurt and milk. Begin and end with the dry ingredients, mixing until just combined.
- Fold in the chopped dried fish (himono) until evenly distributed throughout the batter.

2. Bake the Cake:

- Pour the batter into the prepared cake pan, spreading it evenly with a spatula.
- Bake in the preheated oven for 30-35 minutes, or until a toothpick inserted into the center of the cake comes out clean.
- Remove from the oven and let the cake cool in the pan for 10 minutes. Then transfer it to a wire rack to cool completely.

3. Prepare the Savory Glaze (Optional):

- In a small bowl, whisk together the powdered sugar, soy sauce or tamari, mirin, and water until smooth and well combined.

4. Glaze the Cake (Optional):

- Once the cake has cooled completely, drizzle the savory glaze over the top of the cake, allowing it to drip down the sides.

5. Optional Garnish:

- Sprinkle chopped green onions or chives over the top of the glazed cake for added flavor and decoration.

6. Slice and Serve:

- Slice the Himono Cake into pieces and serve. Enjoy the unique savory twist on traditional cake flavors!

Tips for Making Himono Cake:

- **Dried Fish (Himono):** Choose dried fish that has been finely chopped for easier incorporation into the cake batter. Adjust the amount according to your preference for savory flavor.
- **Savory Glaze:** The savory glaze adds extra depth of flavor to the Himono Cake. Adjust the ingredients to balance the sweetness and savory notes according to your taste.
- **Storage:** Store any leftover Himono Cake in an airtight container in the refrigerator for up to 3 days. Serve chilled or at room temperature.

Himono Cake offers a unique and savory twist on traditional cake recipes, incorporating the umami flavors of dried fish (himono) into a moist and delicious cake. Enjoy making and savoring this distinctive Japanese-inspired dessert!

Yuzu Honey Cake

Cake Ingredients:

- 1 3/4 cups all-purpose flour
- 2 teaspoons baking powder
- 1/2 teaspoon baking soda
- 1/4 teaspoon salt
- 1/2 cup unsalted butter, softened
- 3/4 cup granulated sugar
- 3 large eggs
- 1/2 cup honey
- 1/2 cup plain Greek yogurt
- Zest of 2 yuzu fruits (about 1 tablespoon)
- Juice of 1 yuzu fruit (about 2-3 tablespoons)
- 1 teaspoon vanilla extract

Yuzu Glaze Ingredients:

- 1 cup powdered sugar
- Juice of 1-2 yuzu fruits (about 4-6 tablespoons)
- Zest of 1 yuzu fruit (about 1/2 tablespoon)

Optional Garnish:

- Yuzu slices or zest curls, for decoration

Instructions:

1. Prepare the Cake:

- Preheat your oven to 350°F (175°C). Grease and flour a 9-inch round cake pan or line it with parchment paper.
- In a medium bowl, whisk together the flour, baking powder, baking soda, and salt. Set aside.
- In a large mixing bowl, cream together the softened butter and granulated sugar until light and fluffy.
- Add the eggs one at a time, beating well after each addition. Mix in the honey, Greek yogurt, yuzu zest, yuzu juice, and vanilla extract until well combined.
- Gradually add the dry ingredients to the wet ingredients, mixing until just combined and no lumps remain.

2. Bake the Cake:

- Pour the batter into the prepared cake pan, spreading it evenly with a spatula.
- Bake in the preheated oven for 30-35 minutes, or until a toothpick inserted into the center of the cake comes out clean.
- Remove from the oven and let the cake cool in the pan for 10 minutes. Then transfer it to a wire rack to cool completely.

3. Prepare the Yuzu Glaze:

- In a small bowl, whisk together the powdered sugar, yuzu juice, and yuzu zest until smooth and well combined. Adjust the consistency by adding more yuzu juice if needed.

4. Glaze the Cake:

- Once the cake has cooled completely, drizzle the yuzu glaze over the top of the cake, allowing it to drip down the sides.

5. Optional Garnish:

- Garnish with yuzu slices or zest curls for a decorative touch and added citrus flavor.

6. Slice and Serve:

- Slice the Yuzu Honey Cake into pieces and serve. Enjoy the bright and refreshing flavors of yuzu combined with the sweetness of honey in this delicious dessert!

Tips for Making Yuzu Honey Cake:

- **Yuzu Substitution:** If fresh yuzu fruits are not available, you can substitute with a combination of lemon and lime zest and juice for a similar citrusy flavor.
- **Greek Yogurt:** Greek yogurt adds moisture and a slight tanginess to the cake. You can substitute with sour cream if preferred.
- **Storage:** Store any leftover Yuzu Honey Cake in an airtight container at room temperature for up to 3 days. The flavors may intensify over time, making it even more delicious!

Yuzu Honey Cake offers a unique and refreshing twist on traditional honey cakes, showcasing the aromatic flavors of yuzu citrus. Enjoy making and sharing this delightful Japanese-inspired dessert with family and friends!

Kuzumochi Cake

Cake Ingredients:

- 1 cup kudzu starch (kuzuko)
- 1 1/2 cups water
- 1/2 cup granulated sugar
- 1/4 teaspoon salt
- 1 teaspoon vanilla extract
- 1 tablespoon vegetable oil

Topping (Optional):

- Kinako (roasted soybean flour) for dusting
- Kuromitsu (Japanese brown sugar syrup), for drizzling
- Fresh fruit (such as strawberries or kiwi slices), for garnish

Instructions:

1. Prepare the Kuzumochi Cake Batter:

- In a medium saucepan, combine the kudzu starch (kuzuko), water, granulated sugar, and salt over medium heat.
- Stir continuously until the mixture thickens and becomes translucent, similar to a thick paste or pudding consistency. This process typically takes about 5-7 minutes.
- Remove the saucepan from heat and stir in the vanilla extract and vegetable oil. Mix well until fully incorporated.
- Transfer the mixture into a greased 8x8 inch baking dish or cake pan, spreading it evenly with a spatula.

2. Chill and Set:

- Allow the Kuzumochi cake mixture to cool to room temperature.
- Once cooled, cover the dish with plastic wrap and refrigerate for at least 2 hours, or until the cake is set and firm.

3. Serve:

- When ready to serve, remove the Kuzumochi Cake from the refrigerator.
- Cut into squares or rectangles. Optionally, dust with kinako (roasted soybean flour), drizzle with kuromitsu (Japanese brown sugar syrup), and garnish with fresh fruit slices.

4. Enjoy:

- Serve chilled and enjoy the unique texture and delicate sweetness of Kuzumochi Cake!

Tips for Making Kuzumochi Cake:

- **Kudzu Starch (Kuzuko):** Kuzuko is essential for achieving the unique texture of Kuzumochi Cake. Ensure it is properly cooked and thickened to achieve the right consistency.
- **Chilling Time:** Refrigeration helps the cake set and allows flavors to meld. It also enhances the texture to a firm, jelly-like consistency.
- **Variations:** Experiment with different toppings such as matcha powder for a green tea flavor, or add a scoop of vanilla ice cream alongside for a delightful dessert variation.

Kuzumochi Cake offers a delightful twist on traditional Japanese sweets, highlighting the unique qualities of kudzu starch in a cake form. Enjoy making and savoring this delicate and refreshing dessert!

Japanese Sweet Bean Cake

Cake Ingredients:

- 1 cup all-purpose flour
- 1 teaspoon baking powder
- 1/4 teaspoon baking soda
- 1/4 teaspoon salt
- 1/2 cup unsalted butter, softened
- 3/4 cup granulated sugar
- 2 large eggs
- 1/2 cup whole milk
- 1 teaspoon vanilla extract

Anko Filling Ingredients:

- 1 cup sweet red bean paste (anko)
- 2 tablespoons unsalted butter, softened

Optional Garnish:

- Powdered sugar, for dusting
- Whipped cream or vanilla ice cream, for serving

Instructions:

1. Prepare the Anko Filling:

- In a small bowl, mix together the sweet red bean paste (anko) and softened butter until well combined. Set aside.

2. Prepare the Cake Batter:

- Preheat your oven to 350°F (175°C). Grease and flour an 8-inch round cake pan or line it with parchment paper.
- In a medium bowl, whisk together the flour, baking powder, baking soda, and salt. Set aside.
- In a large mixing bowl, cream together the softened butter and granulated sugar until light and fluffy.
- Add the eggs one at a time, beating well after each addition. Mix in the vanilla extract.
- Gradually add the dry ingredients to the butter mixture, alternating with the milk. Begin and end with the dry ingredients, mixing until just combined.

3. Assemble the Cake:

- Pour half of the cake batter into the prepared cake pan, spreading it evenly with a spatula.
- Spoon the anko filling over the batter, spreading it evenly to cover.
- Carefully spoon the remaining cake batter over the anko filling, spreading it gently to cover the filling completely.

4. Bake the Cake:

- Bake in the preheated oven for 30-35 minutes, or until a toothpick inserted into the center of the cake comes out clean.
- Remove from the oven and let the cake cool in the pan for 10 minutes. Then transfer it to a wire rack to cool completely.

5. Optional Garnish:

- Dust the top of the Japanese Sweet Bean Cake with powdered sugar before serving.
- Serve slices of the cake with a dollop of whipped cream or a scoop of vanilla ice cream for an extra indulgent treat.

6. Slice and Serve:

- Slice the Japanese Sweet Bean Cake into pieces and serve. Enjoy the harmonious blend of fluffy cake and sweet anko filling!

Tips for Making Japanese Sweet Bean Cake:

- **Anko Variation:** Experiment with different types of anko, such as smooth (koshian) or chunky (tsubuan), depending on your preference for texture.
- **Storage:** Store any leftover cake in an airtight container in the refrigerator for up to 3 days. Bring to room temperature before serving for best texture and flavor.
- **Serve Warm:** For a comforting dessert, gently warm slices of the cake in the microwave before serving, especially delicious with a scoop of vanilla ice cream.

Japanese Sweet Bean Cake (Anko Cake) offers a delightful combination of flavors and textures, perfect for enjoying as a dessert or snack with tea. Enjoy making and sharing this traditional Japanese-inspired treat!

Anko (Sweet Red Bean Paste) Cake

Cake Ingredients:

- 1 cup all-purpose flour
- 1 teaspoon baking powder
- 1/4 teaspoon baking soda
- 1/4 teaspoon salt
- 1/2 cup unsalted butter, softened
- 3/4 cup granulated sugar
- 2 large eggs
- 1/2 cup whole milk
- 1 teaspoon vanilla extract
- 1 cup sweet red bean paste (anko)

Optional Garnish:

- Powdered sugar, for dusting
- Fresh berries or whipped cream, for serving

Instructions:

1. Prepare the Cake Batter:

- Preheat your oven to 350°F (175°C). Grease and flour an 8-inch round cake pan or line it with parchment paper.
- In a medium bowl, whisk together the flour, baking powder, baking soda, and salt. Set aside.
- In a large mixing bowl, cream together the softened butter and granulated sugar until light and fluffy.
- Add the eggs one at a time, beating well after each addition. Mix in the vanilla extract.
- Gradually add the dry ingredients to the butter mixture, alternating with the milk. Begin and end with the dry ingredients, mixing until just combined.

2. Incorporate Anko into the Cake:

- Gently fold the sweet red bean paste (anko) into the cake batter until evenly distributed. Be careful not to overmix.

3. Bake the Cake:

- Pour the batter into the prepared cake pan, spreading it evenly with a spatula.
- Bake in the preheated oven for 30-35 minutes, or until a toothpick inserted into the center of the cake comes out clean.
- Remove from the oven and let the cake cool in the pan for 10 minutes. Then transfer it to a wire rack to cool completely.

4. Optional Garnish:

- Dust the top of the Anko Cake with powdered sugar before serving.

- Serve slices of the cake with fresh berries or a dollop of whipped cream for added flavor and presentation.

5. Slice and Serve:

- Slice the Anko Cake into pieces and serve. Enjoy the delightful combination of fluffy cake with the sweet richness of anko!

Tips for Making Anko Cake:

- **Anko Texture:** Depending on your preference, you can use smooth (koshian) or chunky (tsubuan) anko paste. Adjust the amount based on how pronounced you want the anko flavor in the cake.
- **Storage:** Store any leftover Anko Cake in an airtight container in the refrigerator for up to 3 days. Bring to room temperature before serving for best texture and flavor.
- **Serve Warm:** For a cozy dessert, gently warm slices of the cake in the microwave before serving. This enhances the aroma and makes the anko filling slightly gooey.

Anko Cake is a wonderful way to enjoy the classic Japanese flavor of sweet red bean paste in a cake form. It's perfect for tea time, dessert, or any occasion where you want to savor the unique sweetness of anko. Enjoy making and sharing this delicious treat!

Yatsuhashi (Cinnamon Rice Flour Dumpling) Cake

Cake Ingredients:

- 1 1/2 cups rice flour
- 1/2 cup kinako (roasted soybean flour)
- 1 teaspoon baking powder
- 1/2 teaspoon baking soda
- 1/4 teaspoon salt
- 1/2 cup unsalted butter, softened
- 3/4 cup granulated sugar
- 2 large eggs
- 1 cup plain yogurt
- 1 teaspoon vanilla extract
- 1 tablespoon ground cinnamon

Optional Topping:

- Powdered sugar, for dusting
- Kinako (roasted soybean flour), for sprinkling

Instructions:

1. Preheat and Prepare:

- Preheat your oven to 350°F (175°C). Grease and flour an 8-inch round cake pan or line it with parchment paper.

2. Mix Dry Ingredients:

- In a medium bowl, whisk together the rice flour, kinako, baking powder, baking soda, salt, and ground cinnamon. Set aside.

3. Prepare Wet Ingredients:

- In a large mixing bowl, cream together the softened butter and granulated sugar until light and fluffy.
- Add the eggs one at a time, beating well after each addition. Mix in the vanilla extract.
- Gradually add the dry ingredients to the butter mixture, alternating with the plain yogurt. Begin and end with the dry ingredients, mixing until just combined.

4. Bake the Cake:

- Pour the batter into the prepared cake pan, spreading it evenly with a spatula.
- Bake in the preheated oven for 30-35 minutes, or until a toothpick inserted into the center of the cake comes out clean.
- Remove from the oven and let the cake cool in the pan for 10 minutes. Then transfer it to a wire rack to cool completely.

5. Optional Topping:

- Dust the top of the Yatsuhashi Cake with powdered sugar and sprinkle with kinako (roasted soybean flour) before serving.

6. Slice and Serve:

- Slice the Yatsuhashi Cake into pieces and serve. Enjoy the unique flavors of cinnamon and kinako combined in a delightful cake form!

Tips for Making Yatsuhashi Cake:

- **Kinako Variation:** Adjust the amount of kinako according to your preference for its nutty flavor. You can also use it as a topping for extra texture and flavor.
- **Storage:** Store any leftover Yatsuhashi Cake in an airtight container in the refrigerator for up to 3 days. Bring to room temperature before serving for best texture and flavor.
- **Serve Chilled or Warm:** Yatsuhashi Cake can be enjoyed chilled or gently warmed. Warm slices in the microwave for a comforting treat.

Yatsuhashi Cake offers a delightful twist on traditional Japanese flavors, making it a perfect dessert or snack to enjoy with tea or coffee. Enjoy making and savoring this unique and flavorful cake!

Yakimochi (Grilled Rice Cake) Cake

Cake Ingredients:

- 1 1/2 cups glutinous rice flour (mochiko)
- 1/2 cup all-purpose flour
- 1 teaspoon baking powder
- 1/4 teaspoon baking soda
- 1/4 teaspoon salt
- 1/2 cup unsalted butter, softened
- 3/4 cup granulated sugar
- 2 large eggs
- 1 cup coconut milk (or regular milk)
- 1 teaspoon vanilla extract

Optional Topping:

- Shredded coconut, for garnish
- Honey or maple syrup, for drizzling

Instructions:

1. Preheat and Prepare:

- Preheat your oven to 350°F (175°C). Grease and flour an 8-inch round cake pan or line it with parchment paper.

2. Mix Dry Ingredients:

- In a medium bowl, whisk together the glutinous rice flour (mochiko), all-purpose flour, baking powder, baking soda, and salt. Set aside.

3. Prepare Wet Ingredients:

- In a large mixing bowl, cream together the softened butter and granulated sugar until light and fluffy.
- Add the eggs one at a time, beating well after each addition. Mix in the vanilla extract.
- Gradually add the dry ingredients to the butter mixture, alternating with the coconut milk (or regular milk). Begin and end with the dry ingredients, mixing until just combined.

4. Bake the Cake:

- Pour the batter into the prepared cake pan, spreading it evenly with a spatula.
- Bake in the preheated oven for 30-35 minutes, or until a toothpick inserted into the center of the cake comes out clean.
- Remove from the oven and let the cake cool in the pan for 10 minutes. Then transfer it to a wire rack to cool completely.

5. Optional Topping:

- Garnish the top of the Yakimochi Cake with shredded coconut for added texture and flavor. Drizzle with honey or maple syrup if desired.

6. Slice and Serve:

- Slice the Yakimochi Cake into pieces and serve. Enjoy the unique combination of flavors reminiscent of grilled rice cakes!

Tips for Making Yakimochi Cake:

- **Gluten-Free Option:** If you prefer a gluten-free version, use all glutinous rice flour (mochiko) instead of a mix with all-purpose flour.
- **Coconut Variation:** Coconut milk adds a subtle tropical flavor. You can use regular milk for a more traditional taste.
- **Storage:** Store any leftover Yakimochi Cake in an airtight container in the refrigerator for up to 3 days. Warm gently before serving for best texture.

Yakimochi Cake offers a delightful fusion of Japanese tradition and cake indulgence, perfect for enjoying as a unique dessert or treat. Enjoy making and savoring this flavorful and comforting cake!